CHICKEN

by James McNair

Photography by Patricia Brabant
Chronicle Books • San Francisco

Printed in Japan

Library of Congress Cataloging-in Publication Data
McNair, James K.
Chicken.
Includes index.
1. Cookery (Chicken)
I. Title.
TX750.M37 1987 641.6'65 86-29880
ISBN 0-87701-439-6
ISBN 0-87701-411-6 (pbk)

Distributed in Canada by
Raincoast Books
112 East Third Avenue
Vancouver, British Columbia V5T 1C8
10 9 8 7 6

Chronicle Books
San Francisco, California

For my father, J. O. McNair, whose barbecued chicken is the best in the
world, with much love and appreciation.

And in memory of my grandmother, Olivia Belle Keith, whose luscious fried
chicken would have made the Colonel pea green with envy.

CONTENTS

AN INTERNATIONAL FAVORITE

Perfectly roasted chicken is the centerpiece of my favorite brisk-autumn evening meal. This hallmark of good cooking comes hot from the oven, redolent of herbs and garlic, with the mahogany-colored skin crispy and the meat juicy and tender. To my way of thinking, a simple reduction of the roasting-pan juices surpasses any chef's complex sauce. Add some wild rice, garden-fresh vegetables, a bottle of wine, a slow-burning log in the fireplace, and my best dining companion, and I'm blissfully content.

Or is summertime barbecued chicken my all-time favorite? My father, for forty years the Baptist minister in our small Louisiana town, cooks heavenly chicken that's devilishly spicy. The bird is never burned to a cinder on the outside and bloody red near the bone, as I've too often encountered elsewhere. Daddy's rendition stays miraculously succulent inside, while the perfectly charred skin is masked with a thick, sweet but tangy sauce that gives new meaning to the phrase "manna from heaven."

The Colonel would be pea green with envy over the golden brown, juicy fried chicken cooked by my grandmother, Olivia Belle Keith, and Aunt Doris in Jackson, Mississippi. Through the years I've often enjoyed their straightforward approach to this southern tradition. The simply floured chicken is dropped into bubbling lard to seal in the juices quickly and to seal out most of the fat, then the heat is reduced so the bird finishes cooking slowly.

My favorite chicken dishes certainly don't stop with these American classics. I get passionate about chicken with Southeast Asian peanut sauce or fiery Thai-style curries. Asian or Italian pasta paired with chicken is a perfect mating. Moroccan *bisteeya*, layers of thin flaky pastry wrapped around spiced chicken that's been poached in sweet fruit nectars, is one of the world's great chicken preparations.

I propose a toast to the year 2500 B.C.! For it was about this time that the red jungle fowl of Southeast Asia, the ancestor of the modern chicken, was domesticated. Four and a half millennia have yielded us an abundance of chickens and a cornucopia of delectable ways of serving mankind's favorite fowl.

ASSETS

Chicken is a mainstay of my cooking. Even when I dine out, I find myself ordering it more likely than not. My dining habits are way ahead of the national trend, however, which records that chicken is now eaten in the majority of American households once a week.

Through the centuries chicken has played an important role in many of the world's cuisines. Today it is rapidly moving toward supremacy in the American market. Studies show that within the next decade per capita consumption of the lowly chicken could pass that of presently mighty beef.

Considering its assets, there's little wonder that chicken is such a venerable favorite.

CHICKEN IS VERSATILE. No other meat can be cooked in as many interesting ways. Even when chicken is eaten frequently, there's no good reason to become bored. The mild meat absorbs a variety of seasonings, and the cooking methods run the whole gamut of possibilities—baking, barbecuing, boiling, braising, frying, grilling, poaching, roasting, sautéing, simmering, steaming, stewing. Chicken can be casseroled, pâtéd, souped, and stuffed; it can be served hot, at room temperature, or chilled. And lest we forget, the chicken, in addition to meat, gives us vitamin-rich eggs, which are almost as versatile as the bird itself.

CHICKEN IS ECONOMICAL. Just a few decades ago chicken was enjoyed regularly in America only by the wealthy. Its appearance on the table of most households marked a very special occasion. Our poultry industry deserves a big salute for making it affordable and plentiful.

CHICKEN IS READILY AVAILABLE. Every supermarket and grocery store offers chicken, all year long, either fresh or frozen. We can buy birds in a wide variety of sizes, either whole or in parts, with bones in or out.

CHICKEN IS NUTRITIOUS. In addition to being loaded with B vitamins and minerals, chicken is a relatively low-cholesterol source of protein. Most nutritionists agree that protein should comprise about 12 percent of our total daily consumption. Chicken is a healthful source of protein·several times a week.

CHICKEN IS RELATIVELY LOW IN CALORIES. The calories in fats are what should concern us. Chicken contains less fat than even its kin, the turkey, to say nothing of veal, lamb, beef, or pork. Smaller, younger chickens contain less fat than larger, older birds. On any chicken the breast is the least fatty part. If you're watching your cholesterol level or weight, keep in mind that chicken skin contains at least half of the total saturated fats. I'll admit that each of the mouth- watering dishes described in the introduction is prepared with the fattening skin intact. If we remove the skin of the chicken when making the vast majority of dishes, we can occasionally indulge in this crunchy treat. Meanwhile, very few preparations suffer in its absence. Leave the skin on during roasting and broiling to keep the meat moist however; just remove it before eating. Add the skin to the pot for flavor when cooking stocks; before using the stock, be sure to skim off the layer of fat that floats to the top.

BUYING

Whole chickens and chicken parts are available fresh or frozen. All have been graded by the United States Department of Agriculture (USDA). Grade A tags indicate the highest quality. Grade B chickens are of slightly lower quality and therefore less expensive; they are good for slow-cooked dishes.

When choosing fresh chickens, first check the skin for blemishes or discoloration. Normal skin color varies from yellow to white, depending upon what the birds have been fed. Your butcher can guide you as to what color marks a fresh, healthy fowl in your area. Fresh whole chickens, chicken parts, or organ meats have no off-odors and the package trays will be relatively free of liquid.

Free-range chickens are often found only in gourmet markets, natural-foods stores, or quality poultry shops. These birds have been raised outside of cramped cages and generally have more old-fashioned chicken flavor. "Organic" chickens are usually raised by this method, plus they have not been fed extra hormones to fatten them up quickly. Their flavor is frequently a bit gamier than nonorganic free-range birds.

Frozen chickens and chicken parts are available year-round, but of course lack the full flavor of their freshly killed counterparts. When you buy frozen chicken, be sure to check the stamped "pull date" that indicates the last day the chicken should be offered for sale. Check the skin for discoloration or blemishes as you would a fresh chicken. Avoid packages with torn wrappers.

Chicken parts, whether fresh or frozen, may be more expensive than purchasing whole chickens. By selecting parts, however, you avoid paying for pieces you don't use. When shopping for best buys, consider the following guidelines from the USDA showing the percentage of edible meat per chicken and chicken part: whole bird, 51 percent; backs, 42 percent; wings, 50 percent; whole or cut up, 51 percent; legs and thighs, 53 percent; and breasts, 63 percent.

Several butchers have demonstrated to me that ounce for ounce of edible meat, boned breasts and thighs are no more expensive than parts with bones. For those of us with little time for cooking, these boned parts are a far better invention than sliced bread.

STORING

Fresh chicken should be well wrapped and stored in the coldest part of the refrigerator. No more than two days should elapse from time of purchase to cooking. If chicken comes securely enclosed in airtight plastic bags or in prepackaged trays, leave the wrapping intact to prevent excessive handling and loss of moisture. Torn wrappings or butcher paper, however, should be replaced with fresh waxed paper or plastic wrap or sealed in plastic storage bags. When repackaging chicken for the refrigerator or freezer, wash the bird under cold running water and pat it dry to curtail bacteria that grow in moisture.

Frozen chicken purchased for future use should be placed immediately in the home freezer. Fresh chickens or parts bought for freezing should be stored in freezer bags or wrapped tightly in freezer wrap, pressing out as much air as possible before sealing. Package giblets separately. Whether purchased frozen or frozen at home, chicken should be stored no longer than four months.

Thaw frozen chicken in the refrigerator for twenty-four hours or at room temperature for eight hours. When you're in a hurry, place the still-wrapped chicken in a large bowl of cold water; this cuts thawing time in half. Be sure chicken is completely thawed before cooking to prevent the survival of harmful bacteria.

TYPES OF CHICKEN

POUSSIN. Sometimes called "baby chickens," these little birds are killed at 4 to 6 weeks and average about 1 pound. Allow 1/2 to 1 bird per serving. Broil, fry, grill, roast, or sauté.

ROCK CORNISH GAME HEN. Hybrids of the Plymouth Rock hen and Cornish game cock, these 4- to 6-week-old chickens average from 1 to 1-1/2 pounds. Allow 1/2 to 1 bird per serving. Broil, fry, grill, roast, or sauté.

BROILER or FRYER. Although officially broilers are a little younger and smaller than fryers, these names are now often used interchangeably for chickens that are killed at 7 to 9 weeks and average from 2-1/2 to 4 pounds. Allow 1/2 pound per serving. Broil, grill, poach, roast, or sauté.

Chicken parts are usually from fryers. Allow 1/2 pound per serving; if boned, allow 4 to 6 ounces per serving. Broil, fry, grill, poach, or roast.

ROASTER. Bred to be very juicy when cooked, these birds are between 2-1/2 and 5 months when killed and weigh between 5 and 7 pounds. Allow 1/2 pound per serving. Roast.

CAPON. Gelded roosters that retain the tenderness of young chickens, but grow to twice the size. Capons are killed at 4 to 5 months, when they weigh in at 6 to 9 pounds. Allow 1/2 pound per serving. Roasting is the best cooking method.

STEWING or BOILING HEN. Not as easy to find as they were once were, these very fat birds range from 4 to 7 pounds and are about 10 months old. They're prized for making the richest stock, but are also great for stews and simmered dishes.

CUTTING UP

Sometimes butchers take their titles too literally, and the packaged chicken parts you find in markets are not cut and trimmed with care. Cutting up your own chickens becomes easy with a little practice.

There are numerous ways to cut up whole birds. Here is a basic method.

1. Place the chicken, breast side up, on a cutting board. Pull one complete leg away from the body, slice through the skin near the body, then press the leg back until the ball of the thigh joint pops out of its socket. Cut between the ball and socket to remove the leg with thigh attached. Repeat this procedure with the other leg.

2. Cut through the leg at the joint between the thigh and the drumstick to separate the two parts.

3. Move the wing so you can feel the joint where it joins the body. Cut between the ball and socket of this joint, then pull the wing away and cut through the skin to disconnect the wing from the body. Repeat with the second wing.

4. Lay the bird on one side. Beginning at the point where the wing was attached, cut where the breast joins the rib bones to separate the breast from the back. Repeat on the other side.

5. Place the breast, skin side up, on the board. Beginning at the neck end, cut the breast in two by cutting through the wishbone, then cut closely down along each side of the breastbone.

6. If you wish, cut the back crosswise into two pieces at the point where the rib cage ends.

BONING

To bone a whole chicken for stuffing or grilling, place it, breast side down, on a cutting board. Make a cut down the center of the back, following the backbone closely from the neck to the tail of the bird. Working on one side at a time, separate the meat from the skeleton with a very sharp boning knife. Use short, shallow strokes to avoid puncturing the skin and work downwards and outwards, holding the skin and meat away from the skeleton to expose where you are cutting. Leaving as small holes as possible, cut out and discard the wishbones, thigh bones, and wing bones as you come to them. When all the meat is loosened, remove the central skeleton.

To bone a whole breast, cut it in half as described in Cutting Up. If you wish, pull off and discard the skin, as well as the thin membrane that lies between the meat and the skin. Using a small sharp knife, scrape the meat away from the bones. Work carefully to avoid tearing the meat. Pull off or cut away any connecting tissue or fat from the breast meat. Locate the white tendon running through the small fillet section underneath the breast. With one hand, take hold of it where it protrudes (a paper towel allows you to grip it when your hand is sticky). Using a small sharp knife in the other hand, press the blade against the meat where it meets the tendon as you pull it out.

To make breast cutlets, or scallopinis, place boned small breasts between two sheets of waxed paper and pound with a mallet or other flat instrument to a uniform thickness of about one-eighth inch. Remove and pound the tender fillet section separately or leave it attached and tuck it in place underneath the larger section of the breast. Large, thick breasts can be cut in half horizontally. Lay the breast down on the board and hold it flat and still with the palm of one hand. With a sharp knife in the other hand, slice the breast horizontally into two equally thick pieces.

To bone a thigh, make a lengthwise cut from joint to joint down to the bone with a small sharp knife, then scrape the meat away from the bone.

To bone a drumstick, bend the bottom of the drumstick back to snap the bottom joint. Using a small sharp knife, cut through the tendons at the bottom joint, then make a lengthwise incision the full length of the drumstick. Scrape the meat away from the bone.

USING THE RECIPES

The recipes that follow celebrate chicken in both its splendor and its comforting simplicity. A couple of them are time-consuming, but the showy and tasty results are well worth the extra effort. The majority go together quickly, and a number can be made ahead of time, completely or in part.

Many of my recipes have less fats than their traditional versions. Of course, there are also times when I've splurged. Adjust the amounts to your own dietary needs, remembering that plain low-fat yogurt can often substitute for sour cream, sauces can be made with low-fat milk instead of whole milk, and light cream (half- and-half) can fill in for heavy cream without greatly changing the end result of the recipe. I've suggested unsalted butter because I like the flavor, but you may choose to use polyunsaturated margarine. The calories will be the same, but you'll cut down on saturated fats.

Salt is included in the ingredients lists with indications in the directions for salting to taste. Most of us have cut back on salt and add little if any during cooking; it can always be added by diners at the table. The only times I've specified amounts are when salt could not be added after cooking and seems necessary to round out the flavor.

Most of the ingredients listed are readily available everywhere. A few recipes call for ethnic specialties that may be difficult to locate; in such cases, I've suggested alternatives that can approximate the authentic taste. In a few cases, there are no alternatives.

The number of servings a recipe yields is an estimate based on the average appetites of people for whom I cook. Adjust the figure up or down to fit the eating habits of your family or friends.

Before the specific recipes begin, you'll find brief basic guidelines for most of the methods used in chicken cookery.

In keeping with the current American trend toward interchangeable courses, I've chosen not to divide the book into the traditional groupings of appetizers, soups, salads, and main dishes. Most of the preparations can be served as simple one-course meals or part of a more elaborate several-course entertainment.

A dish can be either a main event or merely a starter depending on the size of the portion served and the accompaniments. By adding a salad, hearty bread, and perhaps a dessert, any of the soups, for example, will suffice for a full midday or evening meal. They can also be offered in small portions to open a meal. One or two skewers of grilled chicken are a perfect first course, but several skewers become the centerpiece of a repast rounded out with rice and a steamed or grilled vegetable. Even chicken liver pâté, normally thought of as an appetizer to spread on bite-sized toasts can be a satisfying meal when spread on large pieces of warm toast and eaten with a bountiful green salad.

The dishes are arranged according to cooking method. Scattered throughout the sections are salads and other dishes that are meant to be served chilled or at room temperature. When you're looking for a cold dish, check the index. Some of my groupings are arbitrary because recipes often involve more than one cooking technique. For example, the chicken pies begin with poaching a chicken, then the meat is enclosed in pastry and baked; I've included them under roasting and baking.

Cooking Basics

Before cooking by any method, wash and thoroughly dry the chicken, including the inside cavity if cooking whole. Be sure all pinfeathers (immature feathers still enclosed in hornlike sheaths) have been removed. Pull off and discard excess fat.

BRAISING

Older chickens may be braised, or slowly cooked, in a small amount of liquid for up to 2 hours. Younger chickens can be braised, but are tender in 30 to 40 minutes. In either case, the meat is usually browned before adding the liquid and covering the pot. Cooking may be done on top of the stove or in the oven. Many so-called casseroles are actually braised dishes.

BROILING

This method is best reserved for halves of tender young chickens and for fryer parts. Although you'll miss the smoky aroma and flavor of wood cookery, broiling can pinch hit for grilling in many instances.

Preheat the broiler to moderately hot. Place the chicken on a rack about 3 inches below the flame, and cook on each side, turning twice, until the outside is browned but the inside is still moist and juicy, about 8 to 15 minutes per side. The cooking time will depend on the size of the parts or halves. Boned parts will cook much faster than those containing bones. Baste the chicken occasionally during cooking with butter, oil, or a sauce, if you wish.

CASSEROLES

Casseroles are good make-ahead dishes for parties or for come-and-go family dinners when everyone can't sit down to eat at the same time. Many can be frozen and reheated quite successfully to allow for last-minute meals.

Use chicken parts, fryers, roasters, or stewing hens. The chicken can be browned first, then combined with other ingredients, covered, and cooked either on top of the stove or in the oven until tender. Cooking time will vary from 40 minutes to 1-1/2 hours.

GRILLING OR BARBECUING

Whether over a charcoal or wood fire or the electric grill, this popular method is best suited to small young whole or split chickens or to chicken parts. Marinades or sauces are generally used. If the chicken is marinated in the refrigerator, let it come to room temperature before grilling.

Chicken with its skin intact cooks best over indirect heat in a covered grill, which prevents flare-ups caused by the melting of the skin's fat into the fire. Skinned chicken pieces can be quickly grilled directly over an open fire. Whether you use an open or covered grill, follow your grill manufacturer's instructions for building a fire. Allow the fire to reach the glowing stage before adding chicken.

Place whole chickens, breasts down, in a covered grill with indirect heat, then turn and cook, basting occasionally, until the juices run clear when pierced near the thigh joint, about 20 minutes per pound.

Begin bone-in chicken pieces skin side down in a covered grill, cook for 15 minutes, then turn and cook until the juices run clear, about 20 minutes more. Boned pieces will cook in a total of 8 to 12 minutes.

FRYING

Use only for chicken parts that are battered and seasoned, or dredged with flour, before cooking. Deep-fat frying uses enough cooking fat to submerge the chicken. Frying can also be done in fat that is no more than 1/2 inch deep. Be sure the fat is at the proper temperature before adding the chicken. This immediately "seals" the chicken, preventing absorption of too much of the fat.

Heat vegetable or olive oil, a combination of oil and butter (butter alone will burn unless it is clarified first), or lard (if your arteries can handle it) until hot enough to brown a cube of bread quickly. Add the chicken pieces, a few at a time, and cook until crisp and brown on each side, about 10 minutes total. Reduce the heat so the oil simmers briskly and cook, turning chicken once, until done but still juicy inside, about 20 minutes more.

POACHING

Also called simmering or, erroneously, boiling, this method is best for a stewing hen, although less-fat-rich fryers can be used in a pinch. You get both cooked meat and rich stock or broth. It can also be used for fryers when you need cooked chicken meat, or for breasts that require minimal cooking for cold dishes.

To poach stewing hens or fryers, or to make stock, place the whole or cut-up bird in a large pot with just enough cold water to cover barely (or only half cover for a more concentrated stock). Add vegetables, herbs, and spices as you wish or as the recipe directs. Bring the water to a boil, reduce the heat so the water just simmers, cover, and cook until the meat is very tender when pierced, about 35 minutes per pound. Cool the chicken in the stock, which adds to the flavor of the meat and the liquid. Strain the stock before using it. To remove the fat easily, chill the stock; the layer of fat that rises to the top can then be skimmed away.

To poach chicken breasts, which are called for in many recipes for salads and other cold dishes, place the breasts in just enough cold water, chicken stock, and/or white wine to cover barely. Bring the water to a boil, immediately reduce the heat so the water just simmers, and cook until the breast is tender when pierced but still moist inside, about 12 minutes. The meat should be barely past the pink stage. Remove breasts from the poaching liquid to cool to prevent overcooking. Alternatively, bring the liquid just to the boil, remove the pot from the heat, immerse the breasts in the liquid, and let stand for about 20 minutes.

ROASTING

Roasting uses hot, dry air to cook the chicken. Whether stuffed or left plain, any chicken can be successfully roasted, although poussins, Rock Cornish game hens, roasters, and capons are best. Be sure all pinfeathers are removed, using tweezers to pull them out if necessary. Pull out any fat deposits, then wash the bird inside and out. Pat dry with paper toweling so the skin will crisp properly. Trussing with poultry skewers or string keeps the wings and legs close to the body and prevents any stuffing from coming out.

To truss a chicken with string, position the middle of about 3 feet of cotton string under the chicken's back near the neck end. Holding a length of string in each hand, bring both ends up around the bird and crisscross them over the middle of the breast to secure the wings to the body. Bring each length of string down and around to the back of the leg, pull it tight, and wrap around the end of the drumstick. Cross the strings under the tail to the opposite sides and pull tightly to draw the legs together. Wrap the string around the end of the drumstick once again, then tie tightly between the legs. Cut off excess string.

The cavity can be closed by piercing with metal skewers, alone or in combination with string. Trussing kits containing metal skewers and heavy cotton twine are available in cookware stores.

Set the trussed chicken on a rack inside a roasting pan. Place in a preheated oven and cook, basting frequently with butter or oil, a combination of the two, or the basting mixture in the recipe. Cook the bird until juices run clear when pierced near the thigh joint, about 15 minutes per pound at 425° F., about 20 minutes per pound at 375° F., or 30 minutes per pound at 350° F. Stuffed chickens require slightly longer cooking than unstuffed birds. Be sure to remove the string or metal skewers before serving.

SAUTÉING

Also called pan-frying and similar to stir-frying, this method uses only a fraction of the cooking fat of frying. The chicken is kept in motion by stirring, tossing, or continuous turning and cooks quickly. Because of the rapid-cooking process, chicken should be at room temperature before sautéing.

Heat vegetable or olive oil, or a combination of oil and butter, then add the chicken. The hot fat sears the surfaces of the meat, preventing the loss of moisture. Do not crowd the chicken; room allows for turning and prevents moisture-robbing steam from forming. Some recipes call for a quick sautéing of the meat just to brown it. Once this is done, reduce the heat and add the other ingredients to complete the cooking.

STEAMING

This is an excellent low-fat cooking method and is very satisfactory for preparing chicken to be used in dishes calling for cooked chicken meat. Birds can be steamed whole, although steaming serving pieces is easier. A whole chicken or chicken parts can be arranged directly on a steaming rack, but if you want to retain the cooking juices, place the chicken in a shallow ceramic container atop the rack. When serving steamed chicken with the skin intact, you may brown the chicken pieces briefly before steaming for richer color.

Place chicken, seasonings, and any marinating liquids in a dish set on a rack over boiling water. Cover and steam until tender and thigh juices run clear, about 25 to 30 minutes for breasts, 35 to 45 minutes for dark meat.

Steamed Custard Soup

Steaming turns this delicate soup into a soft, comforting custard known in Japan as *Chawanmushi*. Vary the ingredients with whatever you have on hand.

2 cups homemade chicken stock or canned low-sodium
    broth
4 eggs
4 dried Chinese black mushrooms, soaked in warm water
    for 10 minutes, tough stems removed, then slivered
1/2 cup slivered cooked chicken
2 tablespoons finely chopped green onion
2 teaspoons soy sauce, or to taste
1/2 teaspoon Asian-style sesame oil
1 tablespoon freshly squeezed lemon juice

Place the chicken stock in a saucepan over medium-high heat and bring to a simmer.

Beat the eggs in a small bowl. Add about 1/4 cup of the warm stock to the eggs, continuing to beat. Slowly pour the egg-stock mixture into the rest of the stock, stirring constantly. Stir in the mushrooms, chicken, onion, soy sauce, sesame oil, and lemon juice. Pour into a large covered soup bowl, or cover bowl with foil after adding soup. Alternatively, distribute the soup mixture equally among 4 small individual covered soup bowls, or custard bowls or cups covered with foil. Place bowls on the rack of a steamer set over simmering water; steam until set, about 20 to 30 minutes. The custard should have a soft, silky texture and move slightly when the bowl is shaken.

Serves 4.

Chicken Chowder with Corn

Vegetables and grains flavor and thicken chicken stock which is then turned into a creamy base that's counterpointed by crunchy corn, bites of chicken, and roasted sweet pepper.

1 medium-sized pimiento or other red sweet pepper
1 2-1/2- to 3-1/2-pound fryer
1 cup chopped celery
1 cup chopped leek
1/2 cup brown rice
1/2 cup pearl barley
1/4 cup sesame seeds
About 1 cup homemade chicken stock or canned
    low-sodium broth
1-1/2 cups corn kernels (cut from about 3 ears)
1/2 cup heavy cream
Salt
Freshly ground white pepper

Hold the pepper over an open flame or place under a broiler and turn frequently until charred on all sides. place the pepper in a loosely closed paper bag and set aside until cool, about 15 minutes. Remove the pepper from the bag and rub off blackened skin with your fingertips. Cut pepper in half, remove and discard seeds and veins, and cut into julienne. Reserve.

Place the chicken in a stockpot, add water to cover barely, cover, and cook over medium heat until very tender, about 1-1/2 to 2 hours. Cool chicken in the stock, then strain stock into a clean pot and reserve. Remove and discard skin and bones from the cooled chicken and cut or shred meat into julienne. Reserve.

Meanwhile, add the celery and leek to the stock, cover, and cook over medium heat until soft, about 25 minutes. Add the rice, barley, and sesame seeds, cover, reduce heat to simmer and cook until grains are soft, about 40 minutes. Transfer to a food processor or blender and purée until smooth. Strain through a medium sieve into a saucepan. Add reserved chicken, corn kernels, cream, and enough stock for a thick creamy consistency. Season to taste with salt and pepper. Simmer just until the corn is cooked, about 6 to 8 minutes; do not allow to boil.

To serve, ladle soup into bowls and garnish with roasted pepper strips.

Serves 8 as soup course, or 4 or 5 as main course.

Chicken and Vegetables in Broth

Many cuisines include a version of this one-pot repast. The classic *pot-au-feu* of chicken and beef simmered with vegetables has been a favorite of French peasants for centuries. The broth, often with rice, pasta, or toasted bread added, is presented separately as a first course. A platter of the boiled chicken, meat, and vegetables follows, served with mustard and other condiments. The New England boiled dinner is a variation on the French. Both Latin American and Jewish-American cooks prepare a simpler version of "chicken in a pot," serving the meats and vegetables in the broth.

My recipe calls for everything to be served together in large individual bowls, but you may choose to strain the broth and serve it on its own. In either case, be sure to set out crusty bread for soaking up the rich broth.

2 tablespoons olive oil
1 3-1/2- to 4-pound fryer or stewing hen, quartered
2 pounds boneless beef rib
4 garlic cloves, minced or pressed
3 fresh parsley sprigs
3 fresh thyme sprigs
1 bay leaf
8 to 10 whole black peppercorns
3 quarts homemade beef or chicken stock or canned
    low- sodium broth
1 pound mild or spicy smoked pork sausage
12 pearl onions, or more if desired
8 small carrots
8 small summer squash
16 small new potatoes, or 8 small russet potatoes
Salt
Freshly ground black pepper
2 ears corn, sliced into 1-inch-wide pieces
Fresh parsley, cilantro (coriander), or chervil sprigs
    for garnish
Heavy cream (optional)

Heat the oil in a large pot over medium-high heat, add chicken quarters, and lightly brown on all sides. Remove chicken and reserve. Add the beef, garlic, parsley, thyme, bay leaf, peppercorns, and chicken or beef stock to the pot. Bring to a boil over high heat, skim off any scum, reduce heat to simmer, cover, and cook for 1 hour.

Add the reserved chicken-leg-and-thigh portions, sausage, and pearl onions, and simmer 25 minutes. Add the reserved chicken-breast portions, carrots, squash, and simmer until breast meat is still moist but no longer pink when cut at the thickest part, about 15 to 20 minutes. Test vegetables and meats by piercing with a fork; when each is tender, remove with a slotted spoon to prevent overcooking; reserve.

Meanwhile, place potatoes in a separate pot with water to cover, bring to a boil over medium-high heat, and cook until tender when pierced with a fork, 15 to 20 minutes for new potatoes, or up to 40 minutes for russets. (Cooking the potatoes separately keeps the broth from becoming cloudy.) Drain and reserve.

Skim off and discard any fat from the broth. Season to taste with salt and pepper. Cut chicken, beef, and sausage into serving pieces. Return meats, chicken, and vegetables, including potatoes, to the broth. Add corn, and heat until corn is tender and other ingredients are heated through, about 6 to 8 minutes. Distribute chicken, beef, sausage, and vegetables among individual shallow bowls, then add a ladleful of stock. Garnish with selected herb and serve piping hot. Pass a pitcher of cream.

Serves 8.

VARIATIONS: For a South American flavor, add 1 teaspoon ground cumin, or to taste, along with the beef and use ground cayenne pepper instead of ground black pepper. Pass avocado slices and fresh cilantro (coriander) leaves to add at the table.

For a Jewish-American version, omit the sausage and add small turnips and/or chunks of sweet potato along with the other vegetables; pass prepared horseradish instead of cream.

For New England boiled dinner in a bowl, omit the sausage and add 1 medium-sized Savoy cabbage, cut into 8 wedges, along with the vegetables; pass prepared horseradish instead of cream.

Chicken Gumbo

As a youngster, I often stayed with the Spurlocks when my parents went out of town. I was always thrilled when Margaret Spurlock made her simple chicken gumbo for supper. Here's her recipe, with a few touches of my own. You must add either the okra while cooking the soup or the filé (powdered sassafras leaves) just before serving, as both act as a thickener.

1 2-1/2- to 3-1/2-pound fryer, cut into serving pieces
1/2 cup vegetable oil
1/2 cup all-purpose flour
1 cup chopped onion
1 cup chopped celery
1 cup chopped red or green sweet pepper
1 pound fresh okra, sliced 1/8 inch thick (optional)
2 bay leaves, crushed
1-1/2 teaspoons dried thyme, finely crumbled
Salt
Freshly ground black pepper
Ground cayenne pepper
1 teaspoon filé powder (optional)
2 cups hot cooked brown or white rice
3 or 4 green onions, finely chopped, for garnish
Minced fresh parsley for garnish

Place the chicken in a stockpot, add water to cover barely, and bring to a boil over medium-high heat. Skim off any scum, reduce heat to simmer, cover, and cook chicken until it is very tender, about 1 hour. Remove from the heat and let chicken cool in stock. Lift out chicken and reserve stock. Remove and discard skin and bones. Cut meat into bite-sized pieces and reserve.

To make a roux, place oil and flour in a heavy skillet and cook over medium-high heat, stirring constantly, until the mixture is dark brown (Mrs. Spurlock always said until it was "as dark as an old shoe"), about 30 to 45 minutes. Add the onion, celery, sweet pepper, and okra, if using, and cook until the vegetables are tender, about 15 minutes. Add the vegetable mixture and reserved chicken to the reserved stock and simmer until the meat is heated through, about 15 minutes. Season to taste with salt and black and cayenne peppers. If you did not use okra, remove the pot from the heat and stir in the filé.

To serve, ladle gumbo into individual shallow bowls, add a scoop of cooked rice, and garnish with chopped green onions and/or parsley. Eat with a spoon.

Serves 8 as soup course, or 4 as main course.

Chicken Stock

Flavorful stock is the key to good soups and sauces. Start with a fat hen or use chicken pieces saved from other cooking. Freeze the stock in portions that prove useful to you.

1 4- to 5-pound stewing hen, or 4- to 5-pounds raw or
**   cooked chicken pieces or carcasses, including**
**   raw necks, gizzards, and hearts**
3 to 4 quarts water
4 carrots
2 celery stalks
2 large onions, each studded with 2 whole cloves
2 leeks, split lengthwise and washed (optional)
4 fresh parsley sprigs
2 or 3 fresh thyme sprigs
2 bay leaves
Salt

Place chicken in a heavy stockpot, add enough water to cover by about 2 inches, and bring to a boil over medium heat. Skim to remove any scum that rises to the surface. Add the carrots, celery, onions, leeks, parsley, thyme, bay leaves, and salt to taste. Return to a boil, reduce the heat, cover, and simmer until chicken and vegetables are very tender, about 2 to 3 hours, skimming as necessary. Cool the stock.

Remove any fat on the surface of the cooled stock. Discard the chicken or use for another purpose. Discard the vegetables and herbs and strain the stock. Use immediately, or store in the refrigerator for up to 4 days. To freeze stock for up to 6 months, first chill overnight, then remove all accumulated fat from the top. Pour into small freezer containers and freeze.

Makes about 2 quarts.

NOTE: For a more concentrated stock, boil the stock until it is reduced to about one-third the original volume, cool, and pour into ice cube trays. Freeze until solid, then transfer frozen stock cubes to a plastic freezer bag. Combine the thawed cube with water to reconstitute stock to desired strength.

Spicy Chicken Coconut Soup

Ingredients for this Thai favorite can be found in markets that specialize in foods from Southeast Asia. I've included readily available subsitutes that can approximate authentic flavor.

2 chicken breast halves
1/2 cup slivered fresh lemon, including peel
3 tablespoons fish sauce, or 2 teaspoons low-sodium
    soy sauce
1-1/2 teaspoons chopped fresh hot chili pepper, or to taste
2 green onions, thinly sliced, including part of green top
1-1/2 teaspoons sugar
4 cups unsweetened coconut milk (see note)
2 cups homemade chicken stock or canned low-sodium
    broth
3 teaspoons minced fresh or dried lemon grass,
    or 1 teaspoon grated lemon zest
1 cup fresh or canned whole straw mushrooms, drained,
    or sliced fresh mushrooms
1 tablespoon slivered fresh, frozen, or dried galangal
    root or ginger root

Place the chicken breasts in a skillet or saucepan with just enough cold water to cover. Bring to a boil over medium heat and immediately reduce the heat so water barely ripples. Simmer the breasts uncovered until they are done, about 12 minutes. The meat should be moist and opaque throughout; cook only to just beyond the pink stage. Remove breasts with a slotted spoon and drain well. Cool to room temperature, then remove and discard skin and bones. Cut or shred meat into bite-sized pieces. Reserve.

Combine the slivered lemon, fish sauce, chili pepper, green onion, and sugar in a glass or ceramic bowl and reserve.

Combine the coconut milk, chicken stock, lemon grass or zest, mushrooms, and galangal or ginger root in a saucepan over medium-high heat. Bring to a boil, reduce heat, and simmer uncovered until lemon grass is tender, about 15 to 20 minutes. Add reserved chicken meat and lemon mixture and heat through, about 3 minutes.

Serves 6 to 8 as first course, or 4 as main course.

NOTE: Coconut milk can be purchased in cans on grocery shelves or in the freezer. To make your own unsweetened coconut milk, crack the nut by striking it with a hammer or other blunt instrument firmly on its center. Slip a sturdy knife blade into the crack and pry the coconut halves apart. Drain off the liquid inside the nut; it is a delicious beverage drunk as is. Place the coconut halves in a 250° F oven for about 20 minutes. This will dry the meat slightly and make it easier to lift it away from the shell with the point of a knife. Once you have separated the meat from the shell, peel away the thin brown skin that remains on the white meat. Shred or grate the coconut meat into a bowl. Cover with boiling water and let stand for 30 minutes before straining through cheesecloth; squeeze cloth to extract all the milk. If fresh coconut is not available, use unsweetened dried (desiccated) coconut. Cover 4 cups shredded dried coconut with 6 cups boiling water or scalded milk, let stand until the liquid reaches room temperature, then strain through cheesecloth. If you like a sweeter taste or can't locate fresh or desiccated coconut, dissolve 1 cup of readily available canned cream of coconut in 3 cups hot water.

Cold Poached Chicken Breasts in Peanuts with Curried Yogurt Sauce

In this new twist on Indian-style curry, the usual condiments appear both in the nutty coating and in the slightly sweet curry-scented yogurt sauce. Everything can be done ahead for easy entertaining.

6 boned and skinned chicken breast halves
2 cups fresh coconut milk (see note, page 23), or 1 can
(14 ounces) unsweetened coconut milk

CURRIED YOGURT SAUCE:

2 teaspoons minced fresh ginger root, or to taste
1 garlic clove, minced or pressed
1/4 cup dried currants or raisins
1 cup plain low-fat yogurt
2 tablespoons freshly squeezed lemon or lime juice
2 teaspoons ground coriander seeds
1-1/2 teaspoons ground cumin
2 teaspoons ground turmeric
Salt
Ground cayenne pepper

PEANUT COATING:

3/4 cup chutney of choice
3/4 cup mayonnaise or plain low-fat yogurt,
or a combination
2-1/2 cups finely chopped dry roasted peanuts
Sliced mango, papaya, or other tropical fruit for garnish

To poach the chicken breasts, place them in a skillet or saucepan with the coconut milk. Bring to a boil over medium heat and immediately reduce the heat so coconut milk barely ripples. Simmer breasts uncovered until they are done, about 12 minutes. The meat should be moist and opaque throughout; cook only to just beyond the pink stage. Remove breasts with a slotted spoon and drain well; reserve coconut milk. Cool chicken to room temperature, then chill.

To make the yogurt sauce, place the reserved coconut milk over medium-high heat and boil until it is reduced to about 1 cup. Remove from the heat, add the ginger, garlic, and raisins; set aside to cool. Combine the cooled coconut milk, yogurt, lemon or lime juice, coriander, cumin, turmeric, and salt and cayenne pepper to taste in a food processor or blender and blend well. Refrigerate until just before serving.

To make the peanut coating, combine the chutney and mayonnaise and/or yogurt in a food processor or blender and purée until smooth. Chill.

About 30 minutes before serving, dip the chicken breasts into the chutney mixture to cover well, then roll in the chopped peanuts, patting to cover the chicken completely. Place on a wire rack and chill until serving time.

Spoon some of the yogurt sauce onto each plate and top with 1 or 2 breast halves. Garnish plates with fresh fruit.

Serves 3 to 6.

Cold Sliced Chicken in Tuna Sauce

Based on *vitello tonnato*, the Italian classic that pairs cold veal with tuna sauce, this innovation uses poached chicken breasts at a fraction of the cost. Plan to make it the day before serving to allow time for the flavors to blend.

POACHED CHICKEN:

6 chicken breast halves
1 medium-sized onion, sliced
1 medium-sized carrot, cut into pieces
1 celery stalk, cut into pieces
3 fresh parsley sprigs
2 bay leaves
1 teaspoon whole white peppercorns
Dry white wine for poaching (optional)

TUNA SAUCE:

1 can (7 ounces) tuna fish packed in oil, preferably olive oil
5 or 6 flat anchovy fillets packed in oil, rinsed and
    patted dry
3 to 4 tablespoons drained capers
1 cup virgin olive oil
1/4 cup freshly squeezed lemon juice or
    white-wine vinegar
1-1/2 cups Mayonnaise (recipe follows) or good-quality
    commercial mayonnaise
Salt
Freshly ground white pepper
Thin lemon slices for garnish
Capers for garnish
Fresh parsley leaflets, preferably flat-leaf Italian type, for
    garnish

To poach the chicken breasts, place them in a skillet or saucepan with the onion, carrot, celery, parsley, bay leaves, and peppercorns. Add just enough water and/or wine to cover. Bring to a boil over medium heat and immediately reduce the heat so water barely ripples. Simmer the breasts uncovered until they are done, about 12 minutes. The meat should be moist and opaque throughout; cook only to just beyond the pink stage. Remove breasts with a slotted spoon and drain well. (Alternatively, the breasts may be steamed.) Cool to room temperature, then remove and discard skin and bones. Reserve.

To make the sauce, combine the tuna, anchovies, capers, olive oil, and lemon juice or vinegar in a food processor or blender and blend until smooth. Put the mayonnaise in a mixing bowl and fold the tuna mixture into it. Add salt and pepper to taste.

Slice the chicken breasts on the diagonal into 1/4-inch-thick slices.

Spread a thin layer of the tuna sauce on a platter. Arrange a layer of sliced chicken over the sauce, then cover with more sauce. Continue layering until the chicken and sauce are used, ending with a layer of sauce. Cover tightly with plastic wrap and refrigerate at least overnight or for up to 3 days.

Remove from the refrigerator a few minutes before serving. Garnish with lemon slices, capers, and parsley.

Serves 8 as appetizer, or 4 to 6 as a main course.

Mayonnaise

1 whole egg, at room temperature
2 egg yolks, at room temperature
1 tablespoon Dijon-style mustard
3 tablespoons freshly squeezed lemon juice or
    white-wine vinegar
2 cups safflower or other vegetable oil, or part olive oil
Salt

In a food processor or blender, combine egg, egg yolks, mustard, and lemon juice or vinegar. Blend for about 30 seconds. With the motor running, add oil in a slow, steady stream. When mayonnaise thickens, turn the motor off. With a rubber or plastic spatula, scrape any oil clinging to sides of container and mix gently into mayonnaise. Add salt to taste. Mayonnaise may be refrigerated in a covered container for up to 5 days.

Makes about 2-1/2 cups.

Herbed Chicken Loaf

Clear aspic suspends cooked chicken, ham, celery, and herbs in this showy first course, cold buffet dish, or picnic main event.

**2 2-1/2- to 3-1/2-pound fryers, or 1 4- to 5-pound stewing
      hen, cut into quarters**
1 onion, studded with several whole cloves
2 celery stalks, chopped
2 carrots, chopped
1/2 cup fresh basil leaves
2 to 3 fresh parsley sprigs
1 bay leaf
Salt
Freshly ground black pepper
**About 4 cups homemade chicken stock or low-sodium
      canned broth**
2 teaspoons (2/3 envelope) unflavored gelatin
1/4 cup cold water
1-1/2 cups finely chopped celery, including inner leaves
**1/4 cup minced fresh parsley, preferably flat-leaf
      Italian type**
2 tablespoons snipped chives
1/2 cup fresh basil leaves, cut into thin strips
1/2 pound Black Forest or other flavorful ham, slivered
Whole chives for garnish
Fresh basil leaves for garnish
Tomato roses (formed from tomato peelings) for garnish

Two days before serving, place the chicken in a stockpot with the onion, celery, carrots, whole basil leaves, parsley sprigs, bay leaf, and salt and pepper to taste. Add enough chicken stock to come halfway up the chicken. Bring to a boil over medium-high heat, reduce heat to low, cover, and simmer, turning pieces after 30 minutes, until chicken is tender, about 1 hour. Cool the chicken in the stock. Remove the chicken, discard skin and bones, and store meat in an airtight container in the refrigerator.

Strain the stock into a saucepan and boil, uncovered, over high heat until it is reduced to about 2 cups. Cool and chill.

The day before serving, combine the gelatin and water in a small bowl and let stand until the gelatin is soft, about 5 minutes. Meanwhile, skim off and discard any fat from the top of the chicken stock, place the stock in a saucepan over high heat, and bring to a boil. Remove from the heat, stir in the softened gelatin, and refrigerate.

Place the cooked chicken meat in a food processor and chop finely. Alternatively, put chicken through a meat grinder fitted with a coarse blade. Season to taste with salt and pepper.

In a mixing bowl, combine celery, parsley, chives, and basil strips. Reserve.

Scatter the slivered prosciutto over the bottom of a 9- x 5- x 3-inch loaf pan. Cover with the reserved celery and herb mixture. Spread the reserved chicken evenly over the celery mixture. Pour the stock-gelatin mixture over the chicken and gently press down on the surface of the loaf so the stock rises just to the surface. Cover with plastic wrap and refrigerate overnight.

To serve, dip the mold briefly in hot water, run a knife around the edges, and unmold onto a serving plate. Garnish with chives, basil leaves, and tomato roses. Cut into slices to serve.

Serves 10 to 12 as appetizer, or 6 to 8 as main course.

Chopped Chicken Liver and Gizzards

Skim off and save the layer of chicken fat that forms on cooled stock to make this Jewish classic. Or remove the fat from chicken cavities and render it in a skillet on the stove top or in the oven. If you're avoiding animal fats, use vegetable oil in place of the chicken fat. Use all livers to substitute for the gizzards if you wish. Serve with toast or a good crusty bread such as cornmeal rye.

6 chicken gizzards
4 tablespoons chicken fat
2 cups finely chopped onion
3/4 pound chicken livers, trimmed, or 1 pound chicken
    livers if not using gizzards
3 hard-cooked eggs, chopped
2 teaspoons minced fresh parsley
2 to 3 tablespoons mayonnaise
Salt
Freshly ground black pepper
Fresh parsley, preferably flat-leaf Italian type, for garnish
Toast or crusty bread

Place the gizzards in a small saucepan with water to cover and cook over medium heat until tender, about 30 minutes. Drain and reserve.

Heat 2 tablespoons of the chicken fat in a skillet over medium heat, add the onion, and cook until soft and golden, about 6 to 7 minutes. Reserve.

Heat the remaining 2 tablespoons chicken fat in a skillet over low heat, add the livers, and cook until done but still pink inside, about 4 minutes. Reserve.

Mince about 2 teaspoons of the hard-cooked eggs and reserve for garnish. Combine the remainder of the hard-cooked eggs and the reserved gizzards and livers, along with their cooking fat, in a food processor and blend until smooth. Alternatively, put through a meat grinder. Add the reserved onion, parsley, 2 tablespoons mayonnaise, and salt and pepper to taste and blend well. Add more mayonnaise if needed for proper consistency. Scrape into a serving bowl or mound on a plate. Garnish with reserved hard-cooked egg and parsley leaflet. Serve with toast or bread.

Serves 8 to 10 as appetizer, or 4 to 6 as main course.

Truffled Chicken Liver Pâté

Although the truffles add elegance, this quick-and-easy pâté is wonderful even without them. Serve with cornichons and crusty French bread. You may instead spread or pipe the pâté onto apple, pear, or firm 'Fuyu' persimmon slices or onto small pieces of crisp toast, and then pass them on trays.

5 tablespoons unsalted butter, softened
1-1/2 cups finely chopped onion
1 garlic clove, minced or pressed
1 pound chicken livers, trimmed
1 teaspoon dry mustard
1/2 teaspoon freshly grated nutmeg
1/2 teaspoon salt, or to taste
Freshly ground black pepper or ground cayenne pepper
2 tablespoons brandy or Cognac
2 tablespoons Madeira or sherry
2 fresh or preserved black or white truffles,
    finely chopped (optional)
Sliced truffles for garnish (optional)

Melt the butter in a small skillet or saucepan over medium heat. Add the onion and cook until soft, about 5 minutes. Add the garlic and cook 1 minute longer. Reserve.

Place the livers in a saucepan, add water just to cover, and bring to a boil. Lower the heat and simmer the livers gently until done but still pink inside, about 4 to 5 minutes. Drain and place in a food processor or blender. Add the reserved onion, mustard, nutmeg, salt, pepper to taste, brandy or Cognac, and Madeira or sherry; blend until smooth. Stir in truffles. Pack into a crock or bowl and chill several hours or overnight. Garnish with sliced truffles before serving.

Serves 8 to 10 as appetizer, or 4 to 6 as main course.

Tropical Chicken Salad with Lime Dressing

Cool and refreshing on a warm day.

LIME DRESSING:
1 teaspoon freshly grated lime zest
1/4 cup freshly squeezed lime juice
1 teaspoon crushed dried red chili peppers, or to taste
1 teaspoon ground cumin
1/2 cup vegetable oil
1/4 cup olive oil

6 chicken breast halves
White wine for poaching (optional)
1 cup thinly sliced celery
1 cup finely diced red sweet pepper
1/2 cup finely chopped green onion
2 tablespoons minced fresh cilantro (coriander)
Salt
2 bananas, sliced
1/2 cup unsweetened grated coconut
1/3 cup unsalted dry-roasted peanuts, chopped
Dandelion or other tender greens, washed and dried
Lime wedges for garnish
Tropical flowers for garnish

To make the lime dressing, combine the lime zest and juice, crushed chilies, and cumin in a bowl and blend well. Slowly drizzle in oils, whisking to mix thoroughly. Reserve.

To poach the chicken breasts, place them in a skillet or saucepan with just enough cold water or white wine to cover. Bring to a boil over medium heat and immediately reduce the heat so water barely ripples. Simmer breasts uncovered until they are done, about 12 minutes. The meat should be moist and opaque throughout; cook only to just beyond the pink stage. Remove breasts with a slotted spoon and drain well. (Alternatively, the breasts may be steamed.) Cool to room temperature, then remove and discard skin and bones. Cut meat into long 1/4-inch-wide strips.

Combine the poached-chicken strips, celery, sweet pepper, green onion, and cilantro in a mixing bowl. Add reserved lime dressing and toss well. Add salt to taste. Chill at least 1 hour before serving. Do not store longer than 3 hours to prevent pickling of the chicken by the lime juice.

Just before serving, toss chicken mixture with the sliced bananas and coconut. Serve on dandelion or other greens Sprinkle with peanuts and garnish with lime slices and tropical flowers.

Serves 8 as first course, or 4 to 6 as main course.

Chicken Salad with Hearts of Artichoke and Palm in Garlic Mayonnaise

Quick, easy, and delicious. Stuff into cold cooked artichokes (chokes removed) for a showy presentation.

2 cups Mayonnaise (page 27) or good-quality
       commercial mayonnaise
2 teaspoons minced or pressed garlic, or to taste
2 jars (6 ounces each) marinated artichoke hearts,
       drained, oil reserved, and sliced
5 chicken breast halves
White wine for poaching (optional)
1 can (7 to 8 ounces) hearts of palm, drained and sliced
4 cold cooked artichokes (optional)

In a small bowl, combine the mayonnaise with the garlic and the oil drained from marinated artichokes. Chill.

To poach the chicken breasts, place them in a skillet or saucepan with just enough cold water or white wine to cover. Bring to a boil over medium heat and immediately reduce the heat so water barely ripples. Simmer the breasts, uncovered, until they are done, about 12 minutes. The meat should be moist and opaque throughout; cook only to just beyond the pink stage. Remove breasts with a slotted spoon and drain well. Cool to room temperature, then remove and discard skin and bones. Cut meat into bite-sized pieces.

Combine the chicken, artichoke hearts, hearts of palm, and garlic-flavored mayonnaise. Serve immediately or chill as long as overnight.

Serves 6 to 8 as first course, or 4 as main course.

Japanese Boiled Chicken
with Sesame Dipping Sauce

Eastern tradition truly meets western casualness in this California version of *mizutaki*. The Japanese use chicken on the bone and cook the dish at the table; it's easier to serve and eat when the chicken has been boned and is cooked in the kitchen.

I've eaten this dish with sauces that vary from a simple combination of equal parts lime juice and soy sauce to a long-guarded San Francisco restaurant recipe featuring sour cream and mayonnaise. My version emphasizes sesame seeds and oil, but does add a bit of very nontraditional cream for a smooth consistency. Serve with hot *sake*.

SESAME SAUCE:
1 cup sesame seeds
1/2 cup Asian-style sesame oil
1/2 cup low-sodium soy sauce
2 tablespoons Japanese rice vinegar or freshly squeezed
    lemon juice
1/2 cup heavy cream or sour cream
3/4 cup lightly seasoned homemade chicken stock,
    or 6 tablespoons each canned low-sodium broth
    and water

2 quarts lightly seasoned homemade chicken stock, or 5
    cups canned low-sodium broth and 3 cups water
4 boned and skinned chicken breast halves, cut into
    bite-sized pieces
2 or 3 medium-sized carrots, sliced on the diagonal
6 green onions, sliced on the diagonal into 2-inch pieces
1 small Napa or other Asian-type cabbage (about 1-1/2
    pounds), leaves separated 1 bunch spinach
    (about 1 pound), trimmed
1 pound firm tofu, cut into 1/2-inch dice (optional)
4 to 6 ounces fresh *enoki* mushrooms (slender Japanese
    white mushrooms; optional)
2 to 3 cups hot steamed short-grain brown or white rice

To make the sauce, place the sesame seeds in a heavy pan over medium-high heat and toast, stirring frequently, until golden. Remove from the heat and pour onto a plate to cool.

Combine cooled sesame seeds and sesame oil in a blender or food processor and blend until smooth. Add the soy sauce, vinegar or lemon juice, cream, and stock, and blend until well mixed. Reserve.

Pour the chicken stock into a large pan and place over medium heat. Bring to a boil. Add the chicken, reduce heat to simmer, and cook until chicken is tender but still moist, about 6 minutes. Remove with a slotted spoon and reserve.

Add the vegetables to the simmering stock one type at a time. Cook until just tender, about 5 minutes. Remove with a slotted spoon before adding the next vegetable. Reserve each vegetable in a different bowl. Cook the tofu in the same way until heated through and reserve.

To serve, pour the reserved sesame sauce into 6 individual sauce bowls and place alongside a small bowl of rice at each place setting. Serve the chicken, each vegetable, and the tofu in separate communal bowls, allowing diners to make selections. Eat the chicken, vegetables, and tofu with chopsticks, dipping each bite into the sesame sauce. After eating the chicken and vegetables, ladle some of the hot broth into 6 individual bowls. Add a bit of leftover sauce to the broth and drink the soup.

Alternatively, combine the chicken, vegetables, and tofu in the broth and ladle the mixture into individual bowls. After eating the chicken and vegetables with chopsticks, add some of the leftover sauce to the broth and drink the soup.

Serves 6.

Green Curry, Thai Style

America has finally discovered the fiery cuisine of Thailand, illustrated here in a dish flavored with a pungent green curry paste. Various Thai curry pastes are available in cans at stores that specialize in Southeast Asian foods. Freshly made paste has more exuberant flavor, however, so the recipe includes directions for making your own curry paste.

This paste keeps well. It is a great addition to grill marinades, sautéed dishes, pasta sauces, soups—almost any dish you enjoy on the spicy side. This recipe yields about four times the amount of paste you'll need for the chicken curry.

Ingredients such as unsweetened coconut milk, galangal root, lemon grass, shrimp paste, and fish sauce can be found in markets that specialize in foods from Southeast Asia. Shrimp paste or *kapee* comes in two forms: fresh and packaged in jars, which is rosy pink in color and must be refrigerated after opening, or sun-dried, which is beige to gray and packaged in slabs; anchovy paste is an adequate substitute.

Serve the curry with steamed rice, preferably the fragrant jasmine-infused rice of Thailand.

GREEN CURRY PASTE:
10 fresh small Serrano or other hot green chili peppers
3 medium-sized shallots, coarsely chopped
5 garlic cloves
1 1/2-inch-piece fresh or thawed frozen galangal root or ginger root, chopped
1 stalk fresh or dried lemon grass, bottom part only, chopped, or 1 tablespoon freshly grated lemon zest
2 teaspoons freshly grated lime zest
1 teaspoon fresh shrimp paste, or 1/2 teaspoon anchovy paste
2 teaspoons ground coriander
2 teaspoons freshly grated nutmeg
1 teaspoon ground cumin
1 teaspoon freshly ground black pepper
1/2 teaspoon ground cloves
1/2 teaspoon fennel seeds
1 teaspoon salt
1/2 cup chopped fresh cilantro (coriander)
1/4 cup peanut oil

1/4 cup vegetable oil
6 boned chicken breast halves or 8 boned thighs, cut into bite-sized pieces
2 cups coconut milk (see note, page 23)
3 tablespoons fish sauce, or 1 tablespoon low-sodium soy sauce
Fresh cilantro (coriander) leaves

To make the curry paste, combine the chilies, shallots, garlic, galangal or ginger, lemon grass or zest, and lime zest in a food processor or blender and chop until well mixed. Add the shrimp or anchovy paste, coriander, nutmeg, cumin, black pepper, cloves, fennel, salt, and cilantro. Purée until well blended. Add the oil, a little at a time, puréeing until smooth. Transfer to an airtight container, top with a little peanut oil, and store in the refrigerator. Makes about 1 cup; keeps 3 to 4 weeks.

To make the chicken curry, heat 2 tablespoons vegetable oil in a skillet or saucepan over medium heat, add the chicken, and sauté until lightly browned, about 2 minutes. Remove chicken with a slotted spoon and reserve.

Heat remaining 2 tablespoons oil in the same pan, add about 1/4 cup curry paste, or to taste, and cook 2 to 3 minutes. Stir in the coconut milk and cook about 5 minutes. Add reserved chicken and the fish sauce. Reduce heat to low and simmer until the chicken is tender, about 8 to 10 minutes for breast meat or 12 to 15 minutes for thigh meat. Just before serving, stir in the cilantro leaves and heat briefly.

Serves 6 to 8 as part of a Thai dinner, or 4 as a main course.

Chicken Paprika

For authenticity, serve this Hungarian original over flat, wide egg noodles with braised sweet-and-sour red cabbage on the side.

2 tablespoons unsalted butter
2 tablespoons vegetable oil
1/4 cup chopped onion
1 garlic clove, minced or pressed
2 tablespoons sweet Hungarian paprika, or to taste
1-1/2 cups peeled, seeded, and chopped fresh ripe
    tomatoes, or canned Italian-style crushed tomatoes
    with their juices
1-1/4 cups homemade chicken stock or canned
    low-sodium broth
6 boned and skinned chicken breast halves, or 12 boned
    and skinned chicken thighs
1/3 cup all-purpose flour
1/3 cup light cream (half-and-half) or heavy cream
1/2 cup sour cream
1 tablespoon sherry
Salt
Freshly ground black pepper
3/4 pound flat egg noodles, cooked *al dente*
Sweet Hungarian paprika for garnish
Minced fresh parsley for garnish

Heat the butter and oil in a heavy skillet over medium-high heat, add onion, and cook until soft, about 5 minutes. Stir in the garlic and cook 1 to 2 minutes. Add the paprika, tomatoes, and chicken stock; cover and cook for 10 minutes. Reduce the heat to a simmer, add chicken, cover, and cook until tender but still moist inside, about 30 to 35 minutes. Remove chicken with a slotted spoon and keep warm.

Combine the flour and light cream in a small bowl and stir to mix well. Stir this mixture into the simmering stock and cook, stirring, until thickened, about 10 minutes. Stir in the sour cream, sherry, and salt and pepper to taste; heat until well blended but do not boil. Serve the sauce over the chicken breasts and *al dente* noodles. Garnish with parsley.

Serves 6.

Chicken Thighs with Poppy-Seed Dumplings

Chicken and dumplings, a country-kitchen tradition, differs from region to region. I've included two distinctive preparations, both of which I enjoy. Gail High at Lake Tahoe first served this version to me. Poppy seeds add crunchiness to the biscuitlike dumplings that cook on top of simmering wine-enriched broth.

6 tablespoons (3/4 stick) unsalted butter
12 chicken thighs, preferably boned and skinned
1-1/2 cups chopped onion
6 tablespoons flour
2-1/2 cups homemade chicken stock or canned
    low-sodium broth
1/2 cup dry white wine
Salt
Freshly ground black pepper
1-1/2 cups milk

POPPY-SEED DUMPLINGS:
2 cups cake flour
4 teaspoons baking powder
1 teaspoon salt
2 tablespoons poppy seeds
1 egg, lightly beaten
2/3 cup milk

Melt the butter in a large, heavy, broad-topped pot over medium heat. Add the thighs, a few at a time, and brown well on all sides, about 5 minutes. Remove and keep warm.

Add the onion to the pan drippings that remain from browning the chicken and cook over medium-high heat until soft, about 5 minutes. Stir in the flour and cook, stirring until bubbly, about 2 minutes. Add the chicken stock, wine, and salt and pepper to taste; bring to a boil. Add the milk and reserved chicken, cover, and simmer until chicken is almost tender, about 50 minutes. Skim off and discard any fat that rises to the surface.

To make the dumplings, combine the flour, baking powder, salt, and poppy seeds in a mixing bowl. In a second mixing bowl, combine the egg and milk, then stir into the dry ingredients until evenly moistened. Drop by about 1/4 cup mounds onto chicken. Cook, uncovered, for 10 minutes, then cover and cook for 10 minutes longer, or until dumplings are cooked through. Serve immediately.

Serves 6.

Southern Chicken and Dumplings

This is the kind of dumpling I grew up with—smoother and heavier than the one in the preceding recipe, more like a thick pasta. For this version, I've adapted a recipe that belongs to my good friend Ruth Dosher. She cooks these dumplings in tubs to feed a church "dinner on the grounds." The chicken is cooked in stock to add more flavor to the dumplings.

1 4- to 5-pound stewing hen, cut up
4 cups (1 quart) homemade chicken stock or low-sodium
    canned broth
1 cup chopped onion
1 cup chopped celery
Salt
Freshly ground white pepper
3 cups milk
1 cup heavy cream

DUMPLINGS:
5 cups all-purpose flour
Pinch of salt
1/2 cup vegetable shortening, chilled
About 6 tablespoons water, chilled

Place the chicken in a large, heavy, broad-topped pot. Add stock, onion, celery, and salt and pepper to taste. Bring to a boil over high heat, and skim off any scum. Reduce the heat, cover, and simmer the chicken until very tender, about 2 to 3 hours. Let the chicken cool in the stock. Remove the chicken and skin and bones. Cut or shred the meat into large bite-sized pieces. Strain the stock and return it to the pot.

Add milk and cream to the stock, place over medium-high heat, and bring almost to a boil, then reduce the heat to low and simmer while you make the dumplings.

To make the dumplings, combine the flour and salt in a bowl. Add vegetable shortening and cut in with a pastry blender or a fork until the mixture resembles coarse meal. Add just enough water to make dough the consistency of pie dough. On a lightly floured board, roll out dough in a large rectangle about 1/8 inch thick. Cut the rectangle into strips about 4 inches long and 1-1/2 inches wide.

Bring the chicken stock to a boil and drop in dough strips, a few at a time. When all the dough strips are added, add the boned chicken, reduce the heat to low, and simmer, uncovered, until the dumplings are done, about 35 to 45 minutes. Gently stir only occasionally during cooking, just enough to keep dumplings submerged and to prevent the dumplings on the bottom from sticking to the pot.

Serves 6.

FRIED & SAUTÉED DISHES

Sliced Artichoke-filled Chicken Rolls

Pass these attractive rounds on a platter or arrange three on a plate for a sit-down first course. If desired, serve with your favorite tomato sauce or use the one on page 47.

**1 cup chopped cooked artichoke hearts (see note),
    or 1 package (9 ounces) frozen artichoke hearts,
    thawed**
1 cup freshly grated Parmesan cheese
1/4 cup mayonnaise
2 garlic cloves, minced or pressed
3 tablespoons minced fresh basil
6 boned and skinned chicken breast halves
Salt
Freshly ground white pepper
6 thin slices prosciutto or other flavorful ham
2 tablespoons olive oil
3 tablespoons unsalted butter

Place the artichoke hearts, cheese, mayonnaise, garlic, and basil in a blender or food processor and purée until fairly smooth. Reserve.

Discard tendons and any connecting tissue or fat from the chicken breasts; separate the little fillet and use if for another purpose or leave it attached and tuck it under the larger muscle. Leave small breasts whole; slice thicker ones in half horizontally. Place breast pieces between 2 sheets of waxed paper and pound with a mallet or other flat instrument to a uniform thickness of about 1/8 inch. Season to taste with salt and pepper.

Top each pounded breast with a slice of prosciutto cut to fit the shape of the breast. Spread prosciutto with a thin layer of the artichoke mixture. Roll up jelly- roll style and secure lengthwise with a skewer or toothpicks, or tie crosswise in several places with cotton string or unwaxed dental floss.

Preheat the oven to 350° F.

Heat the olive oil and butter in an ovenproof sauté pan or skillet over medium heat. Add chicken rolls and cook, turning frequently, until lightly browned, about 5 minutes. Transfer the pan to the oven and cook 10 minutes. Remove the chicken from the oven and let stand until just cool enough to handle. Remove the skewers or string. Slice horizontally on a slight diagonal into 1/3-inch-wide pieces. Serve warm or at room temperature, with sauce on the side if desired.

Serves 10 to 12 as appetizer, or 6 as main course.

NOTE: To cook fresh artichoke hearts, cut off the stem and the top one-third of each artichoke, and then remove the coarse outer leaves. As each artichoke is prepared, place it in water to which a bit of fresh lemon juice or vinegar has been added (this prevents discoloration). To cook, drain artichokes, place in a pan, and add water to cover. Bring to a boil and boil until tender when pierced, 25 to 45 minutes, depending upon size. (Alternatatively, steam over boiling water until tender.) Drain, and when cool enough to handle, remove leaves and cut away and discard fuzzy choke. Chop just the hearts for this recipe. Reserve the leaves for another use. You will need approximately 12 very small artichokes or 4 large ones for this dish.

Cajun Chicken Bites with Apricot Mustard

Less caloric than the popular battered and fried chicken tidbits, these morsels can be seasoned to taste with the spice mix that follows or with one of the several commercial mixtures now coming out of Louisiana. The fruity mustard dipping sauce provides a good foil for the hot spices.

CAJUN SPICE MIX:
2 teaspoons ground cayenne pepper
2 teaspoons freshly ground black pepper
1 teaspoon freshly ground white pepper
2 teaspoons dried thyme, finely crumbled
1 tablespoon garlic powder
1 teaspoon salt, or to taste

APRICOT MUSTARD:
1-1/2 cups apricot preserves
6 tablespoons Creole-style or Dijon-style mustard

5 boned and skinned chicken breast halves,
      cut into bite-sized pieces
2 tablespoons unsalted butter
2 tablespoons vegetable oil

To make the spice mix, combine the peppers, thyme, garlic powder, and salt in a small bowl or plastic bag and stir or shake to mix well. Reserve.

To make the apricot mustard, combine the preserves and mustard in a small saucepan over low heat; stir to mix and heat gently until the preserves melt and are thoroughly blended with the mustard. Set aside to cool.

Sprinkle chicken pieces with spice mix and let stand for about 30 minutes.

Heat butter and oil in a sauté pan or skillet over medium-high heat, add chicken pieces, and sauté until just done, about 5 minutes. Remove with a slotted spoon and drain *briefly* on paper toweling. Serve hot with the apricot mustard dipping sauce.

Serves 8 to 10 as appetizer, or 4 or 5 as main course.

Chicken-and-Bulgur Tidbits with Minted Yogurt Sauce

Variations on the theme of patties made of ground meat and bulgur wheat are found throughout the Middle East. Here chicken substitutes for the more common lamb.

MINTED YOGURT:
1 cup plain low-fat yogurt
2 tablespoons freshly squeezed lemon juice
2 garlic cloves, minced or pressed
2 to 3 tablespoons minced fresh mint
Salt

1/2 medium-sized onion, coarsely chopped
2 garlic cloves
4 boned and skinned chicken breast halves, chopped
1 cup fine bulgur wheat (cracked wheat)
2 tablespoons chopped fresh parsley
1/2 teaspoon salt (optional)
1 teaspoon freshly ground black pepper or ground
      cayenne pepper
Vegetable oil for frying

To make the minted yogurt, combine the yogurt, lemon juice, garlic, mint, and salt to taste in a bowl. Chill.

To make the chicken patties, place the onion and garlic in a food processor or blender and mince. Add the chicken and blend until smooth. Add 1 or 2 tablespoons cold water and blend to a smooth paste.

Place the bulgur in a sieve, rinse under cold running water briefly, then squeeze out moisture. Add the bulgur wheat, parsley, salt, and pepper to the chicken mixture and blend until very smooth and moist. Shape by hand into 1-inch balls or ovals, or 2-inch biscuit-shaped patties.

Add vegetable oil to a depth of 1/2 inch in a skillet and place over medium-high heat. When oil is hot, add chicken balls, and fry, turning frequently, until golden brown and crisp, about 5 minutes. Serve hot or at room temperature with minted yogurt for dipping.

Serves 8 as appetizer, or 4 or 5 as main course.

Sautéed Chicken Cakes with Tomato and Sweet Pepper Sauce

Flavorful tomatoes are the key to a tasty sauce that enlivens rounds of chicken. Fashion small patties for appetizers or make larger ones for a main course.

CHICKEN CAKES:
4 boned and skinned chicken breast halves
3 tablespoons unsalted butter
1 cup chopped red sweet pepper
1/2 cup chopped celery
6 green onions, chopped
2 cups unseasoned fine dry bread crumbs, preferably made
**   from French or Italian bread**
2 eggs, lightly beaten
1/2 cup heavy cream or light cream (half-and-half)
2 tablespoons Dijon-style mustard
1/4 cup minced fresh parsley
2 tablespoons minced fresh tarragon, or 2 teaspoons dried
**   tarragon, finely crumbled**
Salt
Freshly ground black pepper
TOMATO AND SWEET PEPPER SAUCE:
4 tablespoons (1/2 stick) unsalted butter
2 shallots, minced
1 red sweet pepper, seeded, deveined, and chopped
6 flavorful ripe tomatoes, peeled, seeded, and chopped
1/4 cup dry white wine
1/4 cup minced fresh tarragon or parsley, or a combination
Salt
Ground cayenne pepper

Vegetable oil for sautéing
Fresh tarragon or parsley sprigs for garnish

To make the chicken cakes, finely chop the chicken breasts. Reserve.

Heat the butter in a sauté pan or skillet over medium- high heat, add the sweet pepper, celery, and green onions, and cook until the vegetables are tender, about 5 to 6 minutes. Transfer to a mixing bowl. Add the reserved chicken, bread crumbs, eggs, cream, mustard, parsley, tarragon, and salt and pepper to taste. Chill for at least 2 hours or as long as overnight.

To make the sauce, heat the butter in a sauté pan or saucepan over medium heat, add the shallots and sweet pepper, and cook until tender, about 5 minutes. Add the tomatoes and cook 6 to 8 minutes. Stir in the wine and cook until the sauce is thick, about 15 minutes. Add tarragon and/or parsley and salt and cayenne pepper to taste. Keep sauce warm. (If made ahead, reheat prior to serving.)

Preheat the oven to 400° F.

For appetizer-sized cakes, shape about 1 tablespoon of the chicken mixture into a round patty about 1/2 inch thick. Use about 2 tablespoons for main-dish-sized patties.

Heat about 2 tablespoons vegetable oil in a sauté pan or skillet over medium-high heat, carefully add the fragile chicken patties, a few at a time, and sauté, turning once, until golden, about 3 to 4 minutes total cooking time. Add oil as needed. Transfer the patties to an ovenproof dish and bake until done, about 6 minutes. Drain well on paper toweling before serving.

To serve, place 2 or 3 chicken cakes on individual plates with the tomato sauce alongside. Garnish with tarragon or parsley sprigs. Alternatively, spoon a dollop of the sauce on top of each appetizer-sized patty, garnish with a leaflet of tarragon or parsley, and pass on a tray.

Serves 8 to 12 as appetizer, or 4 to 6 as main course.

Chicken Scallopini with Lemon and Caper Sauce

A poultry variation on a traditional Italian veal preparation.

6 boned and skinned chicken breast halves
2 tablespoons olive oil
4 tablespoons (1/2 stick) unsalted butter
Salt
Freshly ground black pepper
2 to 3 tablespoons freshly squeezed lemon juice
1 to 2 teaspoons drained capers
2 tablespoons minced fresh parsley
Thin lemon slices for garnish
Parsley leaflets, preferably flat-leaf Italian type,
    for garnish

Discard the tendons and any connecting tissue or fat from the chicken breasts; separate the little fillet and use it for another purpose or leave it attached and tuck it under the larger muscle. Leave small breasts whole; slice thicker ones in half horizontally. Place breast pieces between 2 sheets of waxed paper and pound with a mallet or other flat instrument to a uniform thickness of about 1/8 inch. Set aside.

Heat the oil and 2 tablespoons of the butter in a sauté pan or skillet over medium-high heat. Add chicken scallops and sauté, turning once, until browned, about 4 to 5 minutes total cooking time. Remove chicken to a warm platter, season to taste with salt and pepper, and reserve.

Add the lemon juice and capers to the pan and heat, scraping the bottom of the pan with a wooden spoon to loosen browned bits. Add the remaining 2 tablespoons of butter and stir until melted. Stir in the minced parsley and pour the sauce over the scallops. Garnish with lemon slices and parsley leaflets.

Serves 4 to 6.

Chicken Scallopini with Mushrooms

Chicken breasts can be turned into thin scallopinis and cooked in any recipe that calls for pounded veal. This one was given to me by Gail High.

6 boned and skinned chicken breast halves
5 tablespoons unsalted butter
5 tablespoons olive oil
1/2 pound fresh mushrooms, sliced
2 tablespoons chopped shallots, or 4 green onions, chopped
1/4 cup dry white wine
1/3 cup homemade chicken stock or canned low-sodium
    broth
1/2 cup heavy cream
Salt
Freshly ground black pepper

Discard the tendons and any connecting tissue or fat from the chicken breasts; separate the little fillet and use it for another purpose or or leave it attached and tuck it under the larger muscle. Leave small breasts whole; slice thicker ones in half horizontally. Place breast pieces between 2 sheets of waxed paper and pound with a mallet or other flat instrument to a uniform thickness of about 1/8 inch. Reserve.

Heat 2 tablespoons each of the butter and oil in a skillet or sauté pan. Add the mushrooms and sauté until tender, about 5 minutes. Remove mushrooms with a slotted spoon and reserve.

Heat the remaining 3 tablespoons each of butter and oil over medium-high heat. Add the chicken scallops and sauté, turning once, until browned, about 4 to 5 minutes total cooking time. Remove chicken and reserve.

Add the shallots or green onion to the pan and cook, scraping the pan bottom with a wooden spoon to loosen browned bits, until tender, about 4 minutes. Add the white wine and chicken stock, bring to a boil, reduce heat to simmer, and cook until the liquids are reduced by half. Stir in the cream and season to taste with salt and pepper. Add mushrooms and chicken and simmer to reheat. Serve immediately.

Serves 4 to 6.

Minced Chicken with Lettuce Leaves

One of my favorite Chinese dishes is minced squab that's eaten rolled in lettuce leaves. This is my adaptation, using the dark meat of chicken. Check Oriental markets or the ethnic-foods section of the supermarket for any ingredients you may not have on hand. Serve as one of several dishes in a traditional all-Chinese dinner or alone as a light main course preceded by a soup and followed by fresh fruit.

1 head romaine or iceberg lettuce
6 dried cloud ears, minced, or 6 dried Chinese black
mushrooms
3 tablespoons sesame seeds
5 boned and skinned chicken thighs
2 tablespoons oyster sauce
1 tablespoon soy sauce
1 tablespoon dry sherry
1/2 teaspoon sugar
1/4 cup peanut or vegetable oil
2 green onions, including a little of the green stalks,
minced
1 1/2-inch-piece fresh ginger root, peeled and minced
3/4 cup minced canned water chestnuts
1 teaspoon Asian-style sesame oil
1 teaspoon cornstarch, dissolved in 2 tablespoons cold
chicken stock or water
Salt
Freshly ground white pepper
Sweet red pepper strips for garnish

Separate the lettuce leaves, wash, dry, wrap in a cloth, and chill at least 1 hour.

If using dried cloud ears or dried mushrooms, cover with warm water and let stand for 2 hours. Drain and squeeze out as much liquid as possible. Discard tough stems, mince cloud ears or mushrooms, and reserve.

Put the sesame seeds in a small skillet over medium heat, and toast the seeds, stirring or shaking the pan, until golden, about 5 minutes. Empty onto a plate to cool. Reserve.

Mince the chicken thighs with a sharp knife and reserve.

In a small bowl, combine the oyster sauce, soy sauce, sherry, and sugar. Stir well and reserve.

Arrange all ingredients within easy reach of the stove.

Heat a wok or large sauté pan over high heat for about 30 seconds, add the vegetable oil, and quickly swirl it to coat the surfaces of the pan. Add the minced chicken, green onions, and ginger; stir-fry for 2 minutes over high heat. Add the water chestnuts and reserved cloud ears or mushrooms and stir-fry for another 2 minutes. Add the sesame oil, toasted sesame seeds, oyster sauce mixture, and cornstarch mixture. Stir-fry until well blended and the sauce is slightly thickened, about 1 to 2 minutes. Season to taste with salt and pepper. Transfer to a large platter, garnish with red pepper, and serve immediately, accompanied with chilled lettuce leaves.

To eat, place about 1 tablespoonful of the chicken mixture on a lettuce leaf, roll or fold the lettuce, and eat out of hand.

Serves 6 to 8 as part of a Chinese dinner, or 4 to 6 as main course.

Chicken Breasts with Hot Green Chili Salsa

When there's little time to prepare dinner, I reach for some homemade hot green chili salsa and stir up this quick and satisfying dish. If there's no homemade salsa on hand or if you're in a hurry, use a high-quality commercial salsa. Serve with cooked pasta or rice.

4 boned and skinned chicken breast halves
2 tablespoons vegetable oil
2 tablespoons unsalted butter
1/4 cup Hot Green Chili Salsa (recipe follows), or to taste
1 cup sour cream
Freshly grated Parmesan cheese

Remove the fillet from each chicken breast. Cut the remaining portion of each breast into strips about the same size as the fillet. Reserve.

Combine the oil and butter in a sauté pan or skillet over medium heat, add the chicken fillets and strips, and sauté until lightly browned on all sides, about 5 minutes. Stir in salsa and sour cream, reduce heat to very low, and simmer until the chicken is tender but still moist inside and the sour cream and salsa blend into a thick sauce, about 10 minutes. Pass Parmesan cheese at the table.

Serves 2 to 4.

Hot Green Chili Salsa

Although best when freshly made, this fiery concoction may be stored in the refrigerator for up to a week or frozen for longer storage.

About 8 fresh *tomatillos* (Mexican husk tomatoes), or
    1 can (8 ounces) *tomatillos*
3 or 4 garlic cloves
6 to 10 fresh jalapeño or other hot chili peppers, stemmed
1 cup firmly packed fresh cilantro (coriander) leaves
    and stems
3 tablespoons freshly squeezed lime or lemon juice
2 tablespoons olive or vegetable oil
Salt

If using fresh *tomatillos*, remove and discard husks and stems, place in a saucepan, cover with water, and bring to a boil over medium-high heat. Cook until translucent and almost tender, about 5 minutes. Drain, rinse, and drain again. Reserve. If using canned *tomatillos*, drain and reserve.

Chop the garlic in a food processor or blender. Add the chilies, cilantro, lime or lemon juice, and reserved *tomatillos*. Pureé to a coarse consistency, then stir in the oil and salt to taste.

Makes 2 to 2-1/2 cups.

Chicken Breasts with Red Grapes

More flavorful than the familar chicken Veronique which uses white grapes, this very lovely main dish is also very easy to make. Serve with a steamed seasonal green vegetable and buttered noodles or cooked whole wheat berries.

2 tablespoons unsalted butter
1 tablespoon olive oil
6 boned and skinned chicken breast halves
1/3 cup white zinfandel or other blush wine
1 cup heavy cream
1 tablespoon fresh whole lemon thyme leaves, or
    1 teaspoon dried thyme, finely crumbled
Salt
Freshly ground black pepper
1/2 pound seedless red grapes

Heat the butter and oil in a sauté pan or skillet over medium-high heat, add chicken, and sauté until meat is lightly browned on all sides, about 5 minutes. Add the wine to the pan and bring to a boil, loosening browned bits from bottom of pan with a wooden spoon. Stir in the cream, thyme, and salt and pepper to taste. Reduce the heat to a simmer, cover, and cook until the sauce thickens slightly, about 5 minutes. Stir in the grapes and simmer until grapes are heated through and the chicken is tender but still moist inside, about 5 minutes.

Serves 4 to 6.

ROASTED & BAKED DISHES

Herb, Garlic, and Lemon Roast Chicken

Like so many people, perfectly roasted chicken is one of my favorite meals. There are countless ways to season chickens, stuffed or plain, for roasting. I prefer stuffings, or "dressings" as we call them in the South, cooked in a separate pan alongside the bird.

The roast chicken I like best is fragrant with garlic, lemon, and herbs. This recipe provides two ways to achieve similar results. Stuffing the flavored butter under the skin does indeed impart greater flavor to the meat, but I more often use the quicker method outlined in the variation, which produces an almost equally tasty chicken. The soy sauce makes the skin brown beautifully while having little influence on the flavor. Truss the chicken cavity closed if you wish; I prefer only to tie the legs together and fill the cavity opening with fresh herbs after cooking.

4 tablespoons (1/2 stick) unsalted butter, softened
Minced zest of 2 lemons
5 or 6 garlic cloves, minced or pressed
3 tablespoons minced fresh thyme, or 1 tablespoon
    dried thyme, finely crumbled
2 tablespoons minced fresh rosemary, or 2 teaspoons
    dried rosemary, finely crumbled
2 tablespoons minced fresh sage, or 2 teaspoons
    dried sage, finely crumbled
1 5- to 6-pound roaster or capon
About 2 tablespoons soy sauce
Salt
Freshly ground black pepper
Fresh bay leaves, thyme, rosemary, sage, or parsley
    sprigs for garnish

Preheat the oven to 375° F.

In a small bowl, combine the butter, lemon zest, garlic, thyme, rosemary, and sage; blend well. Reserve.

Wash the chicken and dry thoroughly, inside and out, with paper toweling. Beginning at the neck opening, slip your fingers between the chicken skin and flesh and loosen the skin on one side of the breast, leaving the skin attached at the cavity opening. Using your fingers in the same way, work under the skin of the thigh and leg, leaving the skin attached at the end of the leg. Loosen the skin on the other side of the chicken in the same way. Insert most of the lemon-and-herb butter under the skin with one hand, using the other hand to distribute the butter evenly from the outside. Rub the remaining flavored butter inside the cavity. Pull the skin at the neck over the opening and skewer it or sew it with heavy kitchen thread to the back of the chicken. Tie the legs together with cotton string.

Rub the entire outside surface of the chicken with soy sauce, then sprinkle to taste with salt and pepper. Place on a rack in a roasting pan and roast, uncovered, for 10 minutes. Reduce the heat to 350° F and cook, basting with pan drippings every 15 minutes, until the juices run clear when the thickest part of the thigh is pierced, about 1 hour and 20 minutes to 1 hour and 40 minutes (or 20 minutes per pound) total cooking time. Remove the string, stuff the cavity opening with fresh herbs, and serve hot or at room temperature. Skim and discard fat from pan juices and pass at the table.

Serves 4.

VARIATION: Do not make the lemon-and-herb butter. Rub the chicken skin with soy sauce and season with salt and pepper. Rub the butter over the skin and inside the cavity. Fill the cavity with the whole garlic cloves and 2 lemons, pricked all over to release juices during cooking. Generously sprinkle the skin with the thyme, rosemary, and sage and roast as above.

Chicken Oregano

Some years ago, for one of the first events staged by our fledgling former San Francisco company, Picnic Productions, three good friends helped partner Lin and me prepare eight hundred pieces of this chicken dish in our small kitchen. In spite of that large-scale production, the recipe has remained an old friend. It can be served hot from the oven, but makes such good picnic fare that I usually serve it at room temperature.

2 eggs, lightly beaten
1/4 cup milk
1 cup unseasoned fine dry bread crumbs, preferably
    made from French or Italian bread
3/4 cup freshly grated Parmesan cheese
1-1/2 tablespoons dried oregano, finely crumbled
Salt
Freshly ground black pepper
10 chicken breast halves, thighs, or legs, or a combination

Preheat the oven to 350° F.

In a shallow bowl, stir together the eggs and milk. Combine the bread crumbs, cheese, oregano, and salt and pepper to taste in a separate shallow bowl. Dip the chicken pieces into the egg mixture, then coat with the crumb mixture, patting crumbs so that they adhere to all sides of the chicken. Repeat the dipping and coating if necessary to coat the chicken sufficiently. Place the chicken pieces on a greased baking sheet and bake until the meat is tender and the coating is crisp, about 40 minutes.

Serves 5 or 6.

Ginger Chicken

Stephen Suzeman of San Francisco and South Africa created this dish for a picnic we staged in a California forest. Chicken thighs are preferable for baked dishes because they don't dry out if you should overcook them by a few minutes.

1 4-inch-piece fresh ginger root, peeled and coarsely
    chopped
2 garlic cloves
2 tablespoons chopped fresh parsley
1 tablespoon coriander seeds, crushed in a mortar
Grated zest of 1/2 lemon
Juice of 1/2 lemon
1/4 pound (1 stick) unsalted butter, softened
Salt
Freshly ground black pepper
4 chicken pieces (breast halves or thighs)

Combine the ginger, garlic, and parsley in a food processor or blender and blend until well chopped and mixed. Add crushed coriander seeds, lemon zest and juice, butter, and salt and pepper to taste. Blend until smooth.

Preheat the oven to 350° F.

Using a small sharp knife and your fingers, carefully loosen skin from chicken pieces and distribute about two-thirds of the ginger mixture between the skin and the flesh of the chicken. Place chicken pieces in a baking dish and rub tops with the remaining ginger mixture. Bake, uncovered, until chicken is done, basting occasionally with pan juices, about 30 minutes for breasts or 45 minutes for thighs.

Serves 2 to 4.

VARIATIONS: Instead of the ginger mixture, stuff under the chicken skin any one of the following combinations.

1/4 pound (1 stick) unsalted butter, 1/4 cup Dijon-style mustard, 1/4 cup honey, and grated zest and juice of 1/2 orange.

1/4 pound (1 stick) unsalted butter, 1 tablespoon dried rosemary, finely crumbled, and 1 tablespoon minced or pressed garlic.

1/2 cup plain low-fat yogurt, curry powder to taste, and 1/4 cup chopped chutney of choice.

3 ounces creamy goat's milk cheese, 2 to 3 teaspoons minced sun-dried tomatoes, and 1 teaspoon minced or pressed garlic.

Chicken Breasts Stuffed with Herbs and Cheese

Bologna, Italy is world famous for its sophisticated cuisine, which includes this preparation for stuffed chicken breasts.

8 boned and skinned chicken breast halves
Salt
Freshly ground white pepper
1/4 pound (1 stick) unsalted butter, softened
3 tablespoons minced fresh parsley, preferably flat-leaf
Italian type
2 tablespoons minced fresh oregano, or 2 teaspoons
dried oregano, finely crumbled
1-1/2 tablespoons minced fresh marjoram, or 1-1/2
teaspoons dried marjoram, finely crumbled
1/2 teaspoon freshly grated nutmeg
1/4 pound Fontina or Bel Paese cheese
Flour for dredging
2 eggs, lightly beaten
1 cup unseasoned fine dry bread crumbs, preferably
made from Italian or French bread
Vegetable oil for frying
1/2 cup dry white wine

Discard the tendons and any connecting tissue or fat from the chicken breasts; tuck the little fillet under the larger muscle. Place breasts between 2 sheets of waxed paper and pound with a mallet or other flat instrument to a uniform thickness of about 1/8 inch. Season to taste with salt and pepper. Reserve.

Place butter in a food processor or blender and whip until light and fluffy. Add parsley, oregano, marjoram, and nutmeg and blend well. Reserve.

Cut the cheese lengthwise into 8 equal-sized pieces and place 1 piece crosswide on each reserved chicken piece. Equally distribute about half of the reserved herb butter among the chicken pieces, spreading it over the cheese. Roll the breasts tightly around the cheese. Place the flour, eggs, and crumbs in 3 separate bowls. Dredge the chicken rolls lightly in flour, then dip into beaten eggs, and finally roll in the bread crumbs.

Preheat the oven to 350° F.

Pour vegetable oil to a depth of 1/8 inch in a heavy skillet, heat over medium heat, add the chicken rolls, and cook until lightly browned on all sides, about 5 minutes. Transfer chicken rolls, seam side down, to a flat, ovenproof baking dish.

Melt the remaining herbed butter in a small saucepan, stir in the wine, and pour the mixture over the chicken. Bake, basting occasionally, until the chicken is golden brown and tender, about 15 minutes. Spoon pan drippings over chicken before serving.

Serves 4 to 6.

Creamy Almond Chicken

This memorable creation originated in the kitchen of Kristi Spence. I drain off the sauce, toss it with pasta, and add dollops of both fresh tomato sauce and pesto sauce on top of the pasta. If you wish to follow suit, use your favorite recipes for the sauces.

1/4 pound (1 stick) unsalted butter, melted
2 teaspoons celery salt
1-1/2 teaspoons dried oregano, finely crumbled
2 teaspoons paprika
1-1/2 teaspoons curry powder
Salt
Freshly ground black pepper
8 boned and skinned chicken breast halves
Flour for dredging
3/4 cup sliced roasted almonds
1-1/2 cups light cream (half-and-half) or low-fat milk
1/2 cup sour cream or plain low-fat yogurt
1/4 cup sherry
3/4 pound pasta, cooked *al dente* (optional)
Tomato sauce (optional)
Basil pesto sauce (optional)
Freshly grated Parmesan cheese (optional)

Combine the butter, celery salt, oregano, paprika, curry powder, and salt and pepper to taste. Set aside.

Preheat the oven to 350° F.

Dredge the chicken pieces in flour, then roll them in the flavored butter. Arrange the chicken in an ovenproof dish, scatter the almonds over the pieces, and pour light cream or milk over the top. Cover the dish and bake for 35 minutes.

Uncover the dish and pour the cooking liquid from the pan into a bowl. Whisk the sour cream and sherry into the juices until smooth. Pour the mixture over the chicken and bake, uncovered, until tender when pierced with a fork, about 15 to 20 minutes more. Serve immediately.

Alternatively, pour the sauce over drained pasta and toss to blend. Distribute pasta among individual plates and top with 1 or 2 chicken breasts. Spoon a little tomato sauce and pesto sauce on top of pasta and sprinkle with Parmesan cheese.

Serves 4 to 8.

Chicken Breasts in Wild Mushroom Cream Sauce

When Lin Cotton and I operated our Twin Peaks Grocery in San Francisco, this was the most popular take-out item. We offered the creamy, mushroom-flecked chicken warm for dinner or packed in tins for the freezer. Make an extra batch and freeze it for last-minute elegant dining. Be sure to serve pasta, rice, or another complex carbohydrate for soaking up all of the rich sauce.

3/4 pound fresh wild mushrooms such as *chanterelles*, morels, *porcini*, or *shiitakes*, or 1/4 pound dried wild mushrooms
3/4 cup sherry or port
4 tablespoons (1/2 stick) unsalted butter
1/4 cup all-purpose flour
2 cups light cream (half-and-half)
1 cup sour cream
1 tablespoon fresh whole thyme leaves, or 3/4 teaspoon dried thyme, finely crumbled
Salt
Freshly ground white pepper
8 boned and skinned chicken breast halves
Pink pepperberries (dried fruit of *Schinus molle* tree) for garnish

Chop the fresh mushrooms, combine with sherry or port, and let stand for about 30 minutes. If using dried mushrooms, leave them whole and combine them with the sherry or port; let stand until very soft, about 1 hour. Drain mushrooms, reserving liquid in either case. Strain the sherry from the dried mushrooms through cheesecloth or a paper coffee filter. Rinse dried mushrooms very thoroughly to remove all grit, drain, and squeeze out moisture. Chop and reserve. If using fresh mushrooms, simply set drained chopped mushrooms aside.

Heat the butter in a saucepan over medium heat, add the flour, and cook until bubbly, about 3 to 5 minutes. Add the light cream and the reserved soaking sherry, and cook, stirring constantly with a wooden spoon or wire whisk, until thick, about 10 minutes. Cool slightly, then add sour cream, reserved fresh or dried mushrooms, and salt and pepper to taste; blend well.

Preheat the oven to 325° F.

Arrange the chicken breasts in an ovenproof dish or pan and cover with the mushroom sauce. Cook, uncovered, until breasts are done but still moist inside, 35 to 45 minutes. Garnish with pink pepperberries.

Serves 4 to 6.

Chicken Enchiladas with Green Chili Sauce

While writing this book at Lake Tahoe, Gail High came to me one summer day to ask if I had a recipe for a mild green chili sauce similar to one she'd had in a local cantina. As I wrote down the instructions for my sauce, I thought how good it would taste with chicken and corn tortillas. In a flash I was off to the market for the ingredients that turned into this recipe, which I first enjoyed with Gail, Ken, and Tanya High, and Mary McCoy on that hot summer afternoon under the shelter of a white umbrella.

Dried oregano from Mexico is more intensely flavored than its counterpart from Europe, and is recommended when fresh oregano is unavailable. No matter the source of the dried herb, use the cut-leaf type instead of ground or powdered.

GREEN CHILI SAUCE:
About 24 fresh *tomatillos* (Mexican husk tomatoes),
    or 2 cans (13 ounces each) *tomatillos*
1/4 cup vegetable oil
2 cups chopped onion
6 or 8 fresh Anaheim or other mild green chili peppers, or
    2 cans (7 ounces each) chopped mild chili peppers
3 teaspoons minced or pressed garlic
2 tablespoons minced fresh oregano, or 2 teaspoons
    dried oregano, finely crumbled
2 tablespoons freshly squeezed lemon or lime juice
1 teaspoon sugar, or to taste
Salt
2 cups homemade chicken stock or canned broth
2 bay leaves

CHICKEN FILLING:
1 3- to 3-1/2-pound fryer
2 cups shredded Monterey Jack cheese (about 1/2 pound)
1 tablespoon minced fresh oregano, or 1 teaspoon dried
    oregano, finely crumbled

Vegetable oil for frying
12 corn tortillas
2 cups shredded Monterey Jack cheese (about 1/2 pound)
Avocado slices or guacamole (use a favorite recipe)
    for garnish
Chopped ripe tomato for garnish
Sour cream for garnish
Ripe olives for garnish
Fresh cilantro (coriander) leaves for garnish and passing
Hot Green Chili Salsa (page 53) or a commercial hot
    salsa for passing (optional)

To make the chili sauce, first prepare the *tomatillos*. If using fresh *tomatillos*, remove and discard husks and stems, place in a saucepan, cover with water, and bring to a boil over medium-high heat. Cook until translucent and almost tender, about 5 minutes. Drain, rinse, and drain again. Reserve. If using canned *tomatillos*, drain and reserve.

Heat the oil in a skillet over medium-high heat, add the onion, and cook until soft, about 5 minutes. Transfer to a food processor or blender and add the reserved *tomatillos*, chilies, garlic, oregano, lemon or lime juice, sugar, salt to taste, and 1 cup of the chicken stock. Blend until smooth.

Transfer the *tomatillo* mixture to a saucepan and add the remaining 1 cup chicken stock and the bay leaves. Bring to a boil over medium-high heat, reduce the heat to low, cover, and simmer the sauce until it is slightly thickened and the flavors are well blended, about 30 minutes. Discard the bay leaves. Use the sauce immediately or refrigerate as long as overnight. Reheat before using.

To make the chicken filling, place the chicken in a heavy pot, add water to cover barely, bring to a boil over high heat, and skim off any scum. Reduce heat, cover, and simmer until the chicken is very tender, about 1-3/4 to 2 hours. Cool the chicken in the stock. Remove the chicken and discard skin and bones. (Reserve stock for another use.) Shred or chop chicken into very small pieces. Combine chicken, cheese, and oregano in a bowl. Reserve.

Preheat the oven to 350° F.

Reheat the chili sauce. Pour oil in a skillet to a depth of 1/2 inch and fry tortillas, one at a time, over medium heat for just a few seconds to freshen, then dip immediately and briefly into the chili sauce. Lay each tortilla on a flat surface, spoon 1/3 to 1/2 cup of the filling down the center of each, roll up into a cylinder, and place, seam side down, in an ovenproof dish. Spoon a little of the sauce over the tops of the enchiladas.

Cover the baking dish with foil and bake until chicken filling is heated through, about 15 minutes. Remove the foil, sprinkle the cheese over the enchiladas, and bake until the cheese is melted, about 10 minutes.

To serve, spoon some of the green chili sauce onto each of 6 preheated plates. Arrange 2 hot enchiladas on top of the sauce on each plate and garnish with avocado slices or guacamole, chopped tomato, sour cream, olives, and cilantro. Pass additional cilantro and hot chili salsa at the table.

Serves 6.

Oven Barbecued Citrus-flavored Chicken Drumettes

Old friend Stephen Marcus has made mountains of these tasty treats for parties. "Drumettes," the large joint of the wing that resembles a miniature drumstick, can often be purchased in supermarket packages. In lieu of this, buy whole wings, disjoint them, and reserve the tip and middle joints for the stockpot. Use the Tomato Barbecue Sauce recipe on page 84 or a good-quality bottled sauce.

3/4 cup freshly squeezed orange juice
1/4 cup freshly squeezed lemon juice
1 cup firmly packed brown sugar
2 cups Tomato Barbecue Sauce (page 84), or 1 bottle
**   (18 ounces) all-natural barbecue sauce**
36 to 40 drumettes (about 3 pounds trimmed wings)
3 small oranges, sliced, then slices cut in half
2 to 3 lemons, sliced, then slices cut in half

Combine the orange and lemon juices, sugar, and barbecue sauce in a saucepan over medium heat; cook, stirring occasionally, until sugar melts and flavors are well blended, about 10 minutes.

Preheat the oven to 325° F.

Arrange the wings in rows in a single layer in a shallow ovenproof dish or pan. Alternate orange and lemon slices between the wings. Pour the barbecue sauce over the top, cover with foil, and bake for 1 hour. Remove foil and bake until wings are tender when pierced with a fork and sauce is thick, about 30 minutes more.

Serves 10 to 12 as appetizer, or 6 to 8 as main course.

Sweet and Tangy Chicken

This recipe, which blends sweet and tangy seasonings, is a variation on the all-time favorite chicken dish of the Tad High family, San Francisco. They use breasts, while I find thighs better for baking. Serve with rice pilaf or couscous and squash or other seasonal vegetables.

6 slices bacon
8 boned chicken breast halves or boned thighs
Flour for dredging
1/3 cup honey
3 tablespoons Dijon-style mustard
1 teaspoon curry powder
Salt
Ground cayenne pepper

Cook the bacon in a skillet over medium heat until crisp, about 5 to 8 minutes. Remove with a slotted spoon, reserving bacon drippings in the pan. Drain bacon on paper toweling, then crumble and set aside.

Preheat the oven to 350° F.

Dredge the chicken pieces with flour, shaking off excess. Place the skillet with the reserved bacon drippings over low heat, add the chicken, and cook until pieces are browned on all sides, about 10 minutes. Transfer chicken to an 8-x 8- x 2-inch baking dish. Bake the chicken, uncovered, for 30 minutes.

In a small bowl, combine the honey, mustard, curry powder, and salt and cayenne pepper to taste. Drizzle the mixture over the chicken and bake, uncovered, until tender, about 15 minutes more. Top with crumbled bacon just before serving.

Serves 4 to 6.

Chicken and Peach Crêpes
with Velouté Sauce

Serve this original from college cooking and nutrition instructor Babs Retzer as a brunch or lunch dish. The crêpes can be made ahead and frozen.

CRÊPES:
5 tablespoons all-purpose flour
1/16 teaspoon salt
2 eggs
3/4 cup milk
1 tablespoon unsalted butter, melted and cooled
Additional melted butter for greasing pans

2 cups sliced ripe, firm fresh peaches
Sugar

CHICKEN FILLING:
4 chicken breast halves
Water or dry white wine
1 tablespoon mayonnaise
Salt
Freshly ground white pepper
Juice from sliced peaches as needed

VELOUTÉ SAUCE:
2 tablespoons unsalted butter
2 tablespoons all-purpose flour
1 cup homemade chicken stock or canned low-sodium
    broth
2 tablespoons sherry
2 tablespoons juice from the peaches
Salt
Freshly ground white pepper

Fresh mint sprigs for garnish

To make the crêpes, combine the flour and salt in a mixing bowl. Using a wire whisk, beat in the eggs, one at a time, until very smooth. Gradually whisk in the milk and melted butter. Let the batter stand at room temperature for about 2 hours.

To cook the crêpes, heat a 5-1/2-inch skillet or crêpe pan over medium heat. Brush the bottom and sides of the pan lightly with melted butter. Just when the butter begins to brown, lift the pan off the heat, add a generous tablespoon of batter, and tilt the pan in a circular motion to spread the batter evenly and thinly over the bottom of the pan. If you have too much batter in the pan after the bottom is covered, pour the excess batter back into the bowl. Return the pan to medium heat and cook the crêpe until set and browned on the underside, about 1 minute. Carefully turn the crêpe with a spatula or fingertips, and cook about 30 seconds on the second side. Slide onto a wire rack to cool slightly. Continue to make crêpes, adding butter to the pan as needed. Once the crêpes have cooled, stack the crêpes to keep them moist. You'll need 8 to 10 crêpes in all.

Place the sliced peaches in a bowl and sprinkle with sugar to taste. Set aside until juices are released.

To make the chicken filling, first poach the chicken breasts. Place them in a skillet or saucepan with just enough cold water or white wine to cover. Bring to a boil over medium heat and immediately reduce the heat so water barely ripples. Simmer the breasts until they are done, about 12 minutes. The meat should be moist and opaque throughout; cook only to just beyond the pink stage. Remove breasts with a slotted spoon and drain well. Cool to room temperature, then remove and discard skin and bones. Chop or shred meat into very small pieces. Combine the chicken with the mayonnaise, salt and pepper to taste, and enough juice from the peaches to moisten the mixture.

To make the sauce, melt the butter in a saucepan over medium heat, add the flour, and cook until bubbly, about 3 minutes. Using a wire whisk, blend in the chicken stock and cook until sauce is smooth and thick, about 5 minutes. Add sherry, peach juice, and salt and pepper to taste.

Preheat the oven to 350° F.

To fill the crêpes, place each one, best-looking side down on a flat surface. Place 3 to 4 tablespoons of the filling in a line down the middle of the crêpe, roll up loosely, and place, seam side down, in an ovenproof dish. Drain the peaches and place them around the filled crêpes. Bake until the crêpes are heated through, about 10 minutes. Turn on the broiler. Cover the crêpes and peaches with the velouté sauce and place under the broiler until glazed, about 3 minues.

To serve, remove the crêpes with a spatula and place 2 on each of 4 or 5 preheated plates. Add some of the peach slices to each plate and garnish with fresh mint.

Serves 4 or 5.

Chicken and Spinach Pie in Polenta Pastry

Coarse cornmeal or polenta adds crunchiness to the topping for this unusual rendition of chicken pie. It's good both hot from the oven as a lunch or supper main dish and at room temperature for picnics or snacks. Look for polenta in specialty food shops and some supermarkets. It is traditionally used in northern Italian cooking. Substitute regular-grind yellow cornmeal when polenta is impossible to find.

FILLING:

4 bunches spinach (about 3 pounds), trimmed, or 2 packages (10 ounces each) frozen spinach, thawed
3 tablespoons olive oil
3 tablespoons unsalted butter
1 teaspoon minced or pressed garlic
1/4 cup dried currants or raisins
3 tablespoons pine nuts or slivered blanched almonds
1/4 pound thinly sliced prosciutto, slivered
2 cups chopped cooked chicken
2 eggs, lightly beaten
1 cup heavy cream
Salt
Freshly ground black pepper

PASTRY:

1-1/2 cups all-purpose flour
1/3 cup polenta (coarsely ground yellow cornmeal)
1/2 teaspoon salt
1/4 pound (1 stick) unsalted butter, chilled and cut into small pieces
3 tablespoons vegetable shortening, chilled and cut into small pieces
1 egg, lightly beaten
1/2 cup ice water, or as needed

To make the filling, wash the fresh spinach thoroughly and place in a pot with whatever washing water clings to the leaves. Cook over medium-high heat until tender, about 3 to 5 minutes. Drain well in a sieve, pressing firmly against the spinach to remove all liquid. If using thawed frozen spinach, squeeze out as much liquid as possible. Coarsely chop the spinach with a knife.

Heat the oil and butter in a sauté pan or skillet over medium-high heat and add spinach, garlic, currants or raisins, pine nuts or almonds, and prosciutto. Cook, stirring, until garlic and nuts begin to color, about 5 minutes. Remove from the heat, stir in chicken, eggs, and cream. Add salt and pepper to taste. Reserve.

To make the crust, combine flour, polenta, and salt in a food processor or a bowl. Add the butter and shortening and cut in with a pastry blender or 2 knifes until the mixture resembles coarse meal. Combine the egg and ice water and stir into the dough just until the mixture holds together; add a little more water if mixture is too dry to hold its shape. Gather dough into a ball, wrap in plastic wrap or waxed paper, and refrigerate about 30 minutes.

Preheat the oven to 350° F.

Place two-thirds of the chilled dough on a lightly floured surface. Roll out the dough into a round about 12 inches in diameter and 1/4 inch thick. Wrap the circle loosely around a floured rolling pin and transfer it to a 9-inch pie pan. Carefully unwrap the round and fit it into the bottom and sides of the pan. Spoon the reserved spinach mixture into the pan. Moisten the edge of the dough with water.

Roll out the remaining portion of dough into a round 1/4 inch thick. Transfer it to the pie pan in the same way you did the bottom crust. Carefully unwrap the round and rest it over the filled pie; press the edges of the round against the inside rim of the pan to seal the top crust to the bottom crust. Trim overhanging dough and crimp the crusts together to make an attractive fluted border. Make several slashes in the top crust to allow steam to escape during baking. Bake until the pastry is golden brown, about 45 to 55 minutes.

Serves 8 to 10 as appetizer, or 6 as main course.

Phyllo-wrapped Chicken Bisteeya

The Moroccans call it "food for the gods." In its natural habitat, the flaky sweet-and-savory pie is most often made with pigeon, although chicken makes a divine version. This recipe makes two pies, one of which may be frozen for a future meal.

CHICKEN AND EGG FILLINGS:

2 2-1/2- to 3-1/2-pound fryers, or 1 4- to 5-pound
    stewing hen, cut into quarters
1 cup finely chopped onion
2 teaspoons minced or pressed garlic
1 tablespoon ground cinnamon
2 tablespoons ground turmeric
1 teaspoon ground allspice
1/2 teaspoon ground mace
1/2 teaspoon ground cloves
1/2 teaspoon ground coriander
1 teaspoon ground cumin
1 teaspoon dried thyme, finely crumbled
1/4 cup minced fresh parsley
2 cups apricot nectar
3 cups apple juice
1 teaspoon salt, or to taste
1 teaspoon freshly ground black pepper, or to taste
12 eggs, beaten
3 tablespoons unsalted butter
1 cup chopped blanched almonds
2 tablespoons powdered sugar

32 sheets *phyllo* dough (about 1-1/2 pounds), thawed
    (in the refrigerator) if frozen
3/4 to 1 pound (3 to 4 sticks) unsalted butter, melted
    and cooled
Ground cinnamon for garnish
Sifted powdered sugar for garnish

To prepare the fillings, place chicken pieces, including neck and organ meats except the liver, in a stockpot. Add the onion, garlic, 2 teaspoons of the cinnamon, turmeric, allspice, mace, cloves, coriander, cumin, thyme, parsley, apricot nectar, apple juice, salt, and pepper. If necessary, add a little water to cover the chicken barely. Bring to a boil over high heat and skim off any scum. Reduce the heat to a simmer, cover, and cook until the chicken is very tender and falls off the bone, about 2 to 3 hours. Remove from the heat and cool chicken in stock. Remove the chicken, discard the skin and bones, and cut or shred the meat into small pieces; reserve. Strain the cooled stock into a saucepan. Place the stock over high heat and cook to reduce to about 2 cups. Add eggs, reduce heat, and simmer, stirring constantly with a wire whisk or wooden spoon, until the eggs are thick and creamy, about 15 minutes. Remove from the heat. Using a slotted spoon, remove eggs, leaving behind any stock that has not been incorporated into the cooked eggs, and reserve. Heat butter in a skillet over medium-high heat, add chopped almonds, and cook until almonds are golden. Cool and combine almonds with the powdered sugar and remaining 1 teaspoon cinnamon. Reserve.

Place 1 sheet of *phyllo* on a flat work surface. Keep remaining dough covered with a lightly dampened cloth towel to prevent the dough from drying out. With a wide pastry brush, lightly brush *phyllo* sheet with cooled melted butter to cover completely. Top *phyllo* sheet with a second sheet placed at a 45-degree angle to the first sheet and brush it lightly with butter. Repeat until 8 sheets in all are used and the sheets form a rough circle of dough. Make a second stack of 8 buttered sheets in the same manner.

Reserve half of the almond mixture. Sprinkle half of the remainder on each stack of *phyllo*, forming an 8-inch circle in the middle of each stack. Cover each circle of nuts with about one-quarter of the reserved egg mixture, then top each stack with half of the reserved chicken. Equally divide remaining egg mixture in half and cover the chicken fillings. Top eggs with reserved almond mixture, equally dividing it between the stacks. Bring one side of *phyllo* up and over to cover as much of the filling as possible and brush the top of the dough with butter. Bring the remaining *phyllo* sides up and around the filling, one by one, overlapping and buttering them as you go, until all sides of the *phyllo* have been folded over the filling. Repeat with the second *phyllo* stack.

Preheat the oven to 375° F.

Brush 1 *phyllo* sheet with butter and lay it over the top of a filled *phyllo* pie. Butter and overlay 7 more sheets, positioning them at angles to form a circle of sheets over the filled pie, much as you did for the base. Butter the underside of a section of the top stack and fold it down under the pie. Continue buttering, overlapping, and folding down to form a smooth, slightly hexagonal shape. Repeat with the second pie.

To cook, place the pies on wire racks on baking sheets and bake until golden brown, about 45 minutes to 1 hour. Remove from the oven and generously sprinkle with powdered sugar and ground cinnamon. Serve hot or at room temperature.

Makes 2 pies; each serves 4 to 6 as a first course, or 2 to 4 as main course.

NOTE: To create a Middle Eastern design on the top as shown in the photograph, draw a desired pattern on a sheet of cardboard and cut away the design to form a template. Sprinkle the hot pie with powdered sugar, cover with the template, and sprinkle with ground cinnamon. Carefully remove the template and serve.

Chicken Tamale Pie

This "pie," with a thick cornmeal crust mixed right into the other ingredients, was a specialty of my good friend M. J. Cotton. She called it "President's Pie" because it was a particular favorite of Richard Nixon, whom she entertained during the early days of his political career in California. It's a great way to use up leftover cooked chicken. The cheese topping is my addition.

4 cups (1 quart) chopped fresh ripe tomatoes, or 1 can
     (28 ounces) Italian-style plum tomatoes, with their
     juices
1 can (16 ounces) cream-style corn
3 to 4 teaspoons salt
1 medium-sized onion, chopped
1/2 cup olive oil
1-1/2 tablespoons chili powder, or to taste
1 cup milk
1/2 cup yellow cornmeal
3 eggs, lightly beaten
1 cup pitted ripe olives
2 cups coarsely chopped cooked chicken
1 cup shredded Monterey Jack cheese, mixed with
     1 cup shredded sharp Cheddar cheese
Olive oil for drizzling

Combine tomatoes, corn, salt, onion, olive oil, and chili powder in a large saucepan and cook over medium heat for 15 minutes.

Preheat the oven to 350° F.

In a mixing bowl, stir together the milk, cornmeal, and eggs; add to the tomato mixture and cook, stirring constantly to prevent scorching, until thick, about 15 minutes. Remove from the heat and stir in the olives and chicken.

Pour mixture into a lightly greased shallow ovenproof dish. Top with the cheeses, drizzle with oil, and bake until the pie is firm and the cheese is crusty, 35 to 45 minutes. Serve piping hot.

Serves 6.

Asparagus and Chicken Casserole

In springtime, when fresh asparagus are plentiful, combine them with chicken, mushrooms, and a velvety white sauce in this subtle casserole. For a fancier presentation, consider serving it scooped into puff pastry cups made from a reliable recipe or purchased.

1 4- to 5-pound stewing hen, or 2 2-1/2- to 3-1/2-pound
    fryers
6 cups (1-1/2 quarts) water
2 pounds fresh asparagus
1/4 pound (1 stick) plus 2 tablespoons unsalted butter
1/2 cup all-purpose flour
3 cups homemade chicken stock or canned low-sodium
    broth
1 cup light cream (half-and-half)
3/4 pound fresh mushrooms, chopped
Salt
Freshly ground white pepper
1/2 cup dry white wine, or to taste
1 cup slivered roasted almonds
1-1/2 cup freshly grated Parmesan or Romano cheese

Place the chicken(s) in a stockpot, add water, bring to a boil over high heat, and skim off any scum. Reduce the heat and simmer chicken until very tender, about 2 to 3 hours. Let the chicken cool in the stock. Remove the chicken and discard skin and bones. Cut the meat into bite-sized pieces and reserve.

Snap off and discard the tough ends of the asparagus. Cut the tender spears into 1-inch lengths. Steam the asparagus until *al dente*. Drain and rinse in cold water to halt cooking and preserve color; drain again. Reserve.

Melt 1/4 pound of the butter in a saucepan over medium heat. Stir in the flour, and cook, stirring, until bubbly, about 5 minutes. Add the stock to the flour mixture, using a wire whisk to combine. Stir in the light cream and simmer until smooth and thickened, about 10 minutes. Add the mushrooms, wine, chicken, and salt and pepper to taste.

Preheat the oven to 350° F.

Melt the remaining 2 tablespoons butter in a small skillet over medium heat, add the almonds, and cook until golden, about 5 minutes.
Combine the asparagus and the chicken mixture in a shallow 9- x 13-inch ovenproof dish. Sprinkle with the cheese, and then with the almonds. Bake the casserole until bubbly and cheese is melted, about 30 minutes.

Serves 6 to 8.

Chicken and Pasta Casserole

Ruth Dosher, who hails from my hometown, shared this hearty supper treat that doubles as a great buffet dish. I changed the cheese from processed "cheese food" to the real thing.

1 4- to 5-pound stewing hen, or 2 2-1/2- to 3-1/2-pound
    fryers
6 cups (1-1/2 quarts) water
1 cup chopped celery
1 green sweet pepper, seeded, deveined, and chopped
1 red sweet pepper (or 2 green peppers if red is
    unavailable), seeded, deveined, and chopped
1 cup chopped fresh mushrooms
1 cup pitted ripe olives, whole or sliced
1 cup canned Italian-style plum tomato purée
1 cup tomato paste
1 pound *fusilli* (corkscrews) or other dried pasta
1/2 pound Cheddar cheese, grated
1/2 pound Monterey Jack cheese, grated
1 cup freshly grated Parmesan cheese

Place the chicken(s) in a stockpot, add water, bring to a boil over high heat, and skim off any scum. Reduce the heat, cover, and simmer chicken until very tender, about 2 to 3 hours. Let the chicken cool in the stock. Remove the chicken and discard skin and bones. Cut the meat into bite-sized pieces and reserve.

Strain the stock into a large pot. Add the celery, sweet peppers, mushrooms, olives, tomato purée, and tomato paste to the chicken stock. Cook over medium-high heat for about 30 minutes. Stir in the pasta and cook until *al dente*, about 20 to 25 minutes. Fold in the reserved chicken.

Preheat the oven to 350° F.

Combine the three cheeses in a bowl.

Alternately layer pasta and chicken mixture with mixed cheeses in a large ovenproof dish, ending with a layer of the cheeses. Cook casserole until cheese is melted and bubbly, about 30 minutes.

Serves 8.

Chicken and Sausage Jambalaya

There are almost as many versions of this Cajun variation on Spanish *paella* as there are cooks in southern Louisiana. Back in Baptist seminary days in New Orleans, Ed Broussard taught me this simple but scrumptious recipe for the now-famous Cajun specialty. He always serves it with potato salad and pickled beets.

1/2 pound Cajun-style andouille or other hot smoked pork
sausages
1 2-1/2- to 3-1/2-pound fryer, cut into serving pieces
Salt
Freshly ground black pepper
1 cup chopped onion
1 cup chopped celery
1 teaspoon minced or pressed garlic, or to taste
2 cups long-grain brown or white rice
2 cups homemade chicken stock, canned low-sodium
broth, or water
Minced fresh parsley for garnish

Slice the sausages into bite-sized pieces and place them in a cast-iron dutch oven or other deep heavy pot with water to a depth of about 1 inch. Cook over medium-high heat until the water boils away, about 10 minutes. Continue cooking until sausage slices are lightly browned and fat is rendered, about 8 minutes more. Remove sausage slices with a slotted spoon and reserve. Leave rendered fat in pot.

Salt and pepper the chicken pieces to taste. Cook them in the rendered sausage fat over medium heat until browned, about 5 minutes. Remove and reserve.

Add the onion and celery to the pot and sauté them until they are soft, about 5 minutes. Add the garlic, reserved sausage and chicken, rice, and chicken stock or water. Bring to a boil, reduce the heat to low, cover, and simmer until the water evaporates and the rice is tender, about 15 minutes. Garnish with minced parsley.

Serves 4.

Chicken and Rice

As a teenager in Jonesville, Louisiana, in the 1950s, I was a regular viewer of a very down-home show called "Lookin' at Cookin'," produced by the nearby television station, KNOE-TV. This recipe goes back to that time. In those days, the mushrooms were canned, the garlic was in salt form, and the rice was white. Updated touches make this everyday dish more enjoyable.

2 tablespoons unsalted butter
2 tablespoons olive oil
6 boned and skinned chicken breast halves
6 to 8 green onions, chopped
3/4 cup chopped green sweet pepper
1/2 cup chopped celery
2 or 3 garlic cloves, minced or pressed
1-1/2 cups sliced fresh mushrooms (about 6 ounces)
1 cup long-grain brown rice, preferably basmati
2 cups homemade chicken stock or canned low-sodium
broth
2 tablespoons freshly squeezed lemon juice
Chili powder
Tabasco sauce
Salt
Freshly ground black pepper

Preheat the oven to 350° F.

Heat the butter and olive oil in an ovenproof sauté pan or skillet over medium-high heat, add chicken breasts, and sauté until lightly browned on all sides, about 5 minutes. Remove chicken and reserve.

Add the onions, sweet pepper, and celery to the same pan and sauté until the vegetables are soft, about 5 minutes. Add the garlic and mushrooms and sauté about 2 minutes. Add the rice and stir until well coated. Add the chicken stock, lemon juice, and chili powder, Tabasco, salt, and pepper to taste. Stir to blend. Arrange chicken breasts on top of the rice, cover the pan, and bake until rice is done, all the liquid is absorbed, and the chicken is tender, about 45 minutes to 1 hour.

Serves 4 to 6.

GRILLED DISHES

Grilled Drumsticks with Cumberland Marinade

Even commonplace drumsticks can be turned into glamorous grilled fare. The marinade is inspired by fruity Cumberland sauce, a longtime companion to roasted fowl.

CUMBERLAND MARINADE:
Grated zest of 1 large orange
Grated zest of 1 lemon
1/2 cup freshly squeezed orange juice
2 tablespoons freshly squeezed lemon juice
2 teaspoons Dijon-style mustard
1 cup red-currant jelly
2 tablespoons port
1/4 teaspoon ground ginger
Salt
Ground cayenne pepper

12 chicken drumsticks
1/2 cup sesame seeds
Grated orange zest for garnish

To make the marinade, combine orange and lemon zests and juices, mustard, jelly, port, and ginger in a small saucepan over medium heat. Bring the mixture to a boil, reduce heat, and simmer until jelly is melted and sauce is well blended. Season to taste with salt and cayenne pepper. Cool slightly, then pour over the drumsticks. Marinate at room temperature for 2 hours or in the refrigerator for at least 4 hours (or preferably overnight).

Prepare a moderate charcoal fire in a grill with a cover.

Place the sesame seeds in a small pan over medium heat and toast, stirring frequently, until golden, about 5 minutes. Pour onto a plate to cool.

Remove the drumsticks from the marinade, place on the grill, cover, and cook, turning and brushing occasionally with the marinade, until tender, about 25 to 30 minutes. Sprinkle with toasted sesame seeds before serving.

Serves 8 to 10 as appetizer, or 6 as main course.

Grilled Young Chickens with Raspberry Marinade

Poussins are baby chickens weighing about one pound each. If unavailable, substitute Rock Cornish game hens or the smallest broilers you can find.

RASPBERRY MARINADE:
3/4 cup puréed fresh or frozen unsweetened raspberries
1 cup raspberry vinegar
Grated zest of 1 lemon
1 tablespoon minced shallot or garlic
2 tablespoons minced fresh mint
Freshly ground black pepper
1/3 cup olive oil

4 1-pound poussins, split, or 4 1-1/2-pound Rock Cornish game hens, split
Fresh raspberries for garnish
Chopped mint for garnish

To make the marinade, combine the puréed raspberries, vinegar, lemon zest, shallot or garlic, mint, and black pepper to taste in a small bowl. Whisk in olive oil until well blended.

Place the split chickens in a shallow glass or ceramic container and pour the marinade over them. Marinate at room temperature for 2 hours or in the refrigerator for about 4 hours.

Prepare a moderate charcoal fire in a grill with a cover.

When the coals reach the glowing stage, remove the chicken from the marinade and place, skin side down, over fire. Turn chicken after 10 minutes and cook, basting frequently with the marinade, until the chicken juices run clear when pierced with a fork near the joint, about 25 to 30 minutes total cooking time. Serve hot or at room temperature. Garnish with fresh berries and chopped mint.

Serves 4 to 8.

Grilled Chicken Breast Hoisin

Hoisin sauce, made from soybeans, garlic, and Chinese spices, can be found in Oriental markets and many supermarkets. Its complex, rich flavor is all you need to season pounded chicken breasts for grilling. *Hoisin*'s exotic bouquet goes well with wild rice.

8 boned and skinned chicken breast halves
1-1/2 cups canned *hoisin* sauce

Discard the tendons and any connecting tissue or fat from the chicken breasts; separate the little fillet and use it for another purpose or leave it attached and tuck it under the larger muscle. Leave small breasts whole; slice thicker ones in half horizontally. Place breast pieces between 2 sheets of waxed paper and pound with a mallet or other flat instrument to a uniform thickness of about 1/2 inch.

Place pounded breasts in a shallow glass or ceramic container and cover with the *hoisin* sauce, rubbing it well into all sides of the chicken. Marinate at room temperature for 2 hours or in the refrigerator for at least 4 hours (or preferably overnight). Return the chicken to room temperature before grilling.

Prepare a moderate charcoal fire in an open grill.

Remove the chicken from the sauce and pour the sauce into a small saucepan. Place the pan over low heat.

When the coals have burned down to the glowing stage, place the chicken on the grill and cook, turning once, until crisp on the outside but moist inside, just barely past the pink stage, about 4 to 6 minutes per side. Baste occasionally with the warm *hoisin* sauce during grilling. Serve immediately.

Serves 4 to 6.

Three Marinades for Grilling

This trio of marinades can be used in the same way as the *hoisin* sauce in the preceding recipe.

KOREAN BARBECUE SAUCE:
1 cup soy sauce
1/2 cup sugar
1/4 cup Asian-style sesame oil
2 garlic cloves, minced or pressed
4 to 6 green onions, finely chopped
1 1-inch-piece fresh ginger root, peeled and minced

Combine soy, sugar, sesame oil, garlic, onions, and ginger in a saucepan. Bring to a boil to dissolve sugar and blend the flavors, then cool and pour over chicken in a glass or ceramic container. Marinate at room temperature for 2 hours or in the refrigerator for at least 4 hours (or preferably overnight). Return the chicken to room temperature before grilling.

Makes about 1-1/2 cups (enough for 1 medium-sized chicken or 6 pieces).

PROVENÇAL MARINADE:
1/2 cup Dijon-style mustard
1/4 cup balsamic vinegar or red-wine vinegar
1/4 cup freshly squeezed lemon juice
6 garlic cloves, minced or pressed
2 tablespoons *herbes de provence* (herb mixture of basil, rosemary, and lavender flowers)
1 cup olive oil

Combine mustard, vinegar, lemon juice, garlic, herbs, and olive oil. Pour over chicken in a glass or ceramic container and marinate at room temperature for 2 hours or in the refrigerator for about 4 hours. Return the chicken to room temperature before grilling.

Makes about 2 cups (enough for 1 medium-sized chicken or 6 to 8 pieces).

ORANGE MARINADE:
3 tablespoons Dijon-style mustard
2 tablespoons honey
3 tablespoons soy sauce
Grated zest of 1 orange
2 cups freshly squeezed orange juice
3 tablespoons freshly squeezed lemon juice

Combine mustard, honey, soy, orange zest, and citrus juices in a small bowl. Pour over chicken in a glass or ceramic container and marinate at room temperature for 2 hours or in the refrigerator for at least 4 hours (or preferably overnight). Return the chicken to room temperature before grilling.

Makes about 3 cups (enough for 2 medium-sized chickens or 12 pieces).

Chicken Breast Yakitori

These traditional Japanese skewers can be expanded into a main course when served with rice and miso soup.

MARINADE:
1/2 cup soy sauce
1/2 cup *mirin* (sweet rice wine) or sherry
1/2 cup homemade chicken stock or canned low-sodium broth
1 1-inch-piece fresh ginger root, peeled and finely chopped

6 boned and skinned chicken breast halves, cut into bite-sized pieces
1 or 2 red sweet peppers, seeded, deveined, and cut into 1-inch cubes
12 green onions, cut into 1-inch lengths
Pickled Japanese *shiso* leaves (available at Asian markets) for garnish (optional)

Soak 12 bamboo skewers in water for 30 minutes.

To make the marinade, combine the soy sauce, *mirin*, chicken stock, and ginger in a shallow dish. Reserve.

Prepare a moderate charcoal fire in an open grill or preheat the broiler.

Thread the chicken pieces onto the presoaked skewers, alternating them with pieces of sweet pepper and green onion. Place in the marinade for about 5 minutes.

Grill or broil skewered chicken on one side for about 2 minutes. Brush with the marinade, then grill on second side for about 2 minutes. Continue brushing and grilling until chicken is done but still moist inside, about 6 to 8 minutes total cooking time.

Serve the skewers on *shiso* leaves on individual plates; drizzle with a little of the marinade.

Makes 12 skewers; allow 2 per serving as appetizer, or 4 or more as main course.

Chicken Saté with Peanut Sauce

This Southeast Asia snack is a perennial favorite around my house. For a main dish, serve with steamed rice, salad, and grilled or steamed asparagus or other vegetable.

MARINADE:
1 tablespoon light brown sugar
1 tablespoon curry powder
2 tablespoons crunchy peanut butter
1/2 cup soy sauce

1/2 cup freshly squeezed lime juice
2 garlic cloves, minced or pressed
Crushed dried red chili peppers

6 boned and skinned chicken breast halves, cut into long strips each about 1/2-inch wide

PEANUT SAUCE:
2/3 cup crunchy peanut butter
1-1/2 cups unsweetened coconut milk (see note on page 23)
1/4 cup freshly squeezed lemon juice
2 tablespoons soy sauce
2 tablespoons brown sugar or molasses
1 teaspoon grated fresh ginger root
4 garlic cloves, minced or pressed
Ground cayenne pepper
1/4 cup homemade chicken stock or canned low-sodium broth
1/4 cup heavy cream
Grated lime zest for garnish
Fresh cilantro (coriander) sprigs for garnish

To make the marinade, combine the brown sugar, curry powder, peanut butter, soy sauce, lime juice, garlic, and crushed chilies to taste in a shallow dish. Thread the chicken pieces on bamboo skewers, weaving skewers in and out of meat lengthwise to create a serpentine design. Place the skewers in the soy sauce mixture. Marinate at room temperature for at least 2 hours or in the refrigerator as long as overnight for a more intense flavor.

To make the peanut sauce, combine peanut butter, coconut milk, lemon juice, soy sauce, brown sugar or molasses, ginger, garlic, and cayenne pepper to taste in a saucepan over moderate heat and cook, stirring constantly, until the sauce is as thick as heavy cream, about 15 minutes. Transfer to a food processor or blender and purée briefly. Add chicken stock and cream; blend until smooth. Reserve. (This mixture can be made several hours ahead and refrigerated. Return to room temperature before serving.)

Prepare a moderate charcoal fire in an open grill or preheat the broiler.

Cook the skewered chicken, turning several times and basting with the marinade, over medium-hot coals (or under a broiler) until crispy on the outside but still moist inside, about 6 to 8 minutes. Sprinkle with lime zest and garnish with cilantro leaves. Serve with the room-temperature peanut sauce for dipping.

Makes about 18 skewers; allow 2 per serving as appetizer, or 4 or more as main course.

Barbecued Chicken, Louisiana Style

My daddy's barbecued chicken is the best I've ever eaten. When I was growing up, Mother always made a sauce from scratch similar to the accompanying Tomato Barbecue Sauce. Since the advent of good commercial products, Daddy has concocted an easy sauce with complex flavors. Friends have begged me for the recipe for this "homemade" sauce for years and some "gourmets" are surprised when they learn it's based on commercial products.

BARBECUE SAUCE:
1/4 pound (1 stick) butter
1 cup finely chopped onion
1 bottle (18 ounces) high-quality hickory-flavored or
    hot barbecue sauce
1 bottle (5 ounces) steak sauce
1/4 cup Worcestershire sauce
2 tablespoons soy sauce, or to taste
3 tablespoons honey, or to taste
1 tablespoon brown sugar, or to taste
2 lemons, quartered
3/4 cup freshly squeezed orange juice

3 2-1/2- to 3-pound fryers, quartered
1/4 cup vegetable oil

To make the sauce, heat the butter in a heavy saucepan over medium-high heat and saute the onion until soft, about 5 minutes. Add the barbecue sauce, steak sauce, Worcestershire sauce, soy, honey, brown sugar, lemons, and orange juice. Bring to a boil, reduce the heat to low, and simmer until the mixture is thick and the flavors are well blended, about 30 minutes. Remove and discard lemons.

Prepare a moderate charcoal fire in a grill with a cover.

Place the chicken quarters in a large stockpot with enough water to cover barely. Bring just to a simmer over medium-high heat, then remove chickens and drain well. Brush the chicken quarters with vegetable oil and place over coals, turning to sear both sides. Move seared chicken to the outside edge of the grill, cover the grill, and adjust grill air vents so that they are only one-quarter open. Turn chicken and brush generously with sauce about every 10 minutes. Cook chicken until tender, about 1 to 1-1/2 hours for breast quarters and 1-1/2 to 2 hours for dark meat. Add soaked hickory, pecan, or other aromatic woods to fire to create smoke during cooking, if desired. Reheat any unused sauce and serve with chicken.

Serves 6 hearty appetites, or 12 modest eaters.

Tomato Barbecue Sauce

Vary the seasonings according to taste.

2 tablespoons vegetable oil
1 cup chopped onion
2 or 3 garlic cloves, minced or pressed
2 pounds flavorful ripe tomatoes, peeled, seeded, and
    chopped, or 1 can (28 ounces) Italian-style crushed
    tomatoes with their juices
1 cup tomato catsup
1/2 cup freshly squeezed lemon juice
1/2 cup cider vinegar
3 tablespoons brown sugar or honey, or to taste
1 tablespoon soy sauce
2 tablespoons Worcestershire sauce
3 or 4 whole cloves
1 teaspoon ground cinnamon
Crushed dried red chili peppers
Salt

Heat the oil in a saucepan over medium heat, add the onion, and cook until soft, about 5 to 8 minutes. Add the garlic and cook 1 minute. Add tomatoes, lemon juice, tomato catsup, vinegar, brown sugar or honey, soy sauce, Worcestershire sauce, cloves, cinnamon, and crushed chilies and salt to taste. Bring to a boil, reduce heat to low and simmer, stirring frequently, until the sauce is very thick, about 2 hours.

Makes about 1 quart (enough for 4 or 5 medium-sized chickens).

Smoked Chicken Salad
with Blueberry Dressing

Smoked chickens can be purchased at gourmet markets or prepared according to the adjacent recipe.

BLUEBERRY DRESSING:
1 tablespoon Dijon-style mustard
3 tablespoons blueberry-flavored wine vinegar
1 teaspoon sugar
Salt
Freshly ground black pepper
1/3 cup virgin olive oil

About 4 cups small leaves of mixed young lettuces,
     spinach, and other garden greens, or a combination
     of spinach leaves and watercress sprigs
1/2 cup pecans
1 apple, cored and thinly sliced (optional)
1/2 red onion, thinly sliced and separated into rings
4 slices bacon
2 cups shredded smoked chicken
Fresh blueberries

Preheat the oven to 350° F.

To make the salad dressing, combine the mustard, vinegar, sugar, and salt and pepper to taste in a small bowl; whisk in olive oil until well blended. Reserve.

Trim the spinach and watercress. Wash leaves, dry, wrap in a cloth towel, and chill.

Place pecans in a small ovenproof pan and toast in the oven, stirring frequently, until lightly browned, about 15 minutes. Pour onto a plate to cool, then chop and reserve.

Arrange chilled greens on 4 individual plates. Top with apple slices, onion rings, and the chopped pecans.

Cook the bacon in a skillet over medium heat until crisp, about 5 to 8 minutes. Remove with a slotted spoon, reserving bacon drippings in the pan. Drain bacon on paper toweling, then crumble and set aside.

Heat bacon drippings over medium heat, add shredded chicken, and heat through. Remove chicken with a slotted spoon and arrange on top of salad greens. Add reserved salad dressing to pan drippings, heat to combine flavors, then drizzle over salads. Serve immediately.

Serves 4 as salad; 2 as main course.

Cold-smoked Chicken

If you enjoy the flavor of smoked chicken, a special smoker will prove to be a worthy addition to the outdoor kitchen. Cold smoking makes food last longer and imparts a smokier flavor than hot smoking. The pan juices that collect in the smoker can be reduced to make a tasty sauce. Use the same proportions with any liquid or favorite marinade and herbs and spices of choice.

2 cups white wine
1/4 cup fresh rosemary
2 or 3 garlic cloves, minced or pressed
Salt
Freshly ground black pepper
3 3- to 3-1/2-pound fryers

In a bowl, combine the wine, rosemary, garlic, and salt and pepper to taste; pour over the chickens in a glass or ceramic container, cover, and refrigerate overnight, turning occasionally to coat with the marinade.

Following instructions in your smoker manufacturer's manual, prepare a fire with charcoal and presoaked aromatic hardwood chips. Position the smoker pan under the grill.

Remove the chickens from the marinade and pour the marinade into the smoker pan. Position the chickens on a rack over the liquid and cook slowly for up to 10 hours, adding more coals and presoaked wood chips every 45 minutes to 1 hour.

Serves 6 hearty appetites, or 12 modest eaters.

Chicken Boudin Blanc

This is a variation on a recipe for "white pudding" that was given to me by Earl Daggett, a former customer at my Twin Peaks Grocery who now demonstrates cooking at The Emporium in San Francisco. Slice and serve with assorted mustards as an appetizer. For a main event, serve whole sausages with grilled polenta slices and mixed grilled vegetables.

1/2 cup vegetable oil
8 cups thinly sliced onion
2 cups day-old fine bread crumbs
3 cups light cream (half-and-half)
1-1/2 pounds very lean white veal, chopped
1-1/2 pounds boned and skinned chicken breast meat, chopped
Generous 1/4 teaspoon ground allspice
Generous 1/4 teaspoon freshly grated nutmeg
Generous 1/4 teaspoon ground ginger
Generous 1/4 teaspoon ground cinnamon
3 tablespoons minced fresh parsley
2 tablespoons salt
3/4 teaspoon freshly ground white pepper
3 whole eggs
9 egg whites
1-1/2 cups heavy cream
About 1/2 pound large sheep sausage casings, soaked in warm water until soft
Milk for poaching
Melted unsalted butter for grilling

Heat the vegetable oil in a large pot over medium-high heat. Add the onion, cover, and cook over low heat until onion is very soft, about 25 minutes. Reserve.

Combine the bread crumbs and light cream in a saucepan over medium-high heat. Bring to a boil, stirring constantly, and cook until the mixture is thickened enough to hold its shape. Reserve.

Combine the veal and chicken in a food processor or blender with the reserved onion, allspice, nutmeg, ginger, cinnamon, parsley, salt, and pepper. Blend until the mixture is very smooth. (Alternatively, put the mixture through a food grinder 3 times.) Transfer the mixture to a large mixing bowl and beat with an electric mixer for 2 minutes. Add whole eggs and beat 2 minutes more. Add egg whites and beat 3 minutes. Divide the mixture into 2 or more batches if necessary to ease handling. Beat in the crumb mixture, then add the heavy cream, a little at a time, and beat until smooth.

With a sausage-stuffing cone or large funnel, stuff casings with the mixture to form sausages about 5 inches long, tying off links with cotton string as you go. Refrigerate overnight.

Prick the chilled sausages in several places and place in a pan with equal parts milk and water just to cover. Bring to a simmer over low heat and poach very gently for about 20 minutes. Drain and refrigerate 3 to 4 days, or freeze in plastic bags for up to 6 months.

Prepare a moderate charcoal fire in an open grill or preheat the broiler.

To cook, separate links and brush with melted butter. Grill over hot coals or under a preheated broiler until done, about 12 to 15 minutes.

Makes about 20 sausages; allow 1/2 per serving as appetizer, or 2 per serving as main course.

Stuffed Chicken Breasts in Mayonnaise Coulée with Two Spirited Aspics

For a brief time caterer Jody Purcell and I had a party production company. Our biggest event was a dinner for almost seven hundred given by clothier Wilkes Bashford to honor designer Ralph Lauren. We featured a showy cold entree that was developed by Scottie McKinney, the San Francisco caterer's caterer, which admirably shared the spotlight with a fashion show staged by Broadway's Michael Bennett.

The showstopping recipe appears complex, but really is only moderately difficult because it is put together in steps that need not be done in rapid succession. And almost everything is completed hours before serving. Serve as a warm-weather main course with crisply cooked vegetables, perhaps tied into individual bundles with chives.

HARD WHITE WINE AND SPIRITS ASPIC:
1 tablespoon (1 envelope) unflavored gelatin
1/2 cup cold water
1/2 cup dry white wine
2 tablespoons clear spirits such as gin or vodka

HARD COGNAC ASPIC:
1 tablespoon (1 envelope) unflavored gelatin
1 cup cold homemade chicken stock or low-sodium
    canned broth
2 tablespoons Cognac

STUFFED CHICKEN BREASTS:
1 pound lean ham, finely ground
1/4 cup Dijon-style mustard
1/3 cup dried currants, soaked overnight in 1/2 cup Cognac
1/3 cup chopped walnuts
2 tablespoons minced green onion
8 boned and skinned chicken breast halves
Salt
Freshly ground black pepper

MAYONNAISE COULÉE:
1 tablespoon (1 envelope) unflavored gelatin
1 tablespoon water
2 cups Mayonnaise (page 27) or good-quality commercial
    mayonnaise

WINE ASPIC COATING:
1 envelope (1 tablespoon) unflavored gelatin
1 cup water
3/4 cup dry white wine
Fresh herbs such as chives, cilantro (coriander), dill,
    tarragon, or thyme
Edible flowers such as borage, citrus, garlic, nasturtiums,
    jasmine, roses, violas, or violets from pesticide-free
    plants, well rinsed to remove dust and insects

The day before you plan to serve this dish, make the two hard aspics. To make the wine and spirits aspic, combine the gelatin and water in a small saucepan and let stand until the gelatin is soft, about 5 minutes. Place over medium heat and stir until the gelatin dissolves, about 2 minutes. Remove from the heat, add the wine and the spirits, pour into a shallow bowl or pan, and refrigerate until just before serving.

To make the Cognac aspic, combine the gelatin and 1/2 cup of the chicken stock in a small saucepan and let stand until the gelatin is soft, about 5 minutes. Place over medium heat and stir until the gelatin dissolves, about 2 minutes. Remove from the heat and add the remaining 1/2 cup chicken stock and the Cognac. Pour into a shallow bowl or pan and refrigerate until just before serving.

Early on the day of serving, prepare the chicken and make the mayonnaise coulée.

To stuff the chicken breasts, first combine the ham, mustard, drained soaked currants, walnuts, and green onion; mix well and reserve.

Prepare a moderate charcoal fire in an open grill.

Discard the tendons and any connecting tissue or fat from the chicken breasts and tuck the little fillet under the larger muscle. Place the breasts between 2 sheets of waxed paper and flatten slightly with a mallet or other flat instrument to a thickness of 1/4 inch. Divide the reserved ham mixture evenly between the 8 pieces, placing it in a row down the middle of each breast. Fold each breast around the mixture and secure with toothpicks or tie with cotton string or unwaxed dental floss. Sprinkle with salt and pepper to taste. Grill over medium-hot coals, turning once, until done but still moist inside, about 15 to 20 minutes. (Alternatively, bake the chicken in an oven preheated to 350° F. Cool chicken and reserve.)

To make the mayonnaise coulée, stir together the gelatin and water and let stand until the gelatin is soft, about 5 minutes. Blend well into the mayonnaise and chill until the mixture thickens to spreading consistency, about 15 minutes.

Place the cooled chicken breasts on a wire rack sitting on a shallow-rimmed tray and spoon the mayonnaise coulée over them to form a smooth coating. Chill until firm, about 30 minutes.

To make the wine aspic coating, combine the gelatin and 1/2 cup of the water in a small saucepan and let stand until the gelatin is soft, about 5 minutes. Place over medium heat and stir until the gelatin dissolves, about 2 minutes. Remove from the heat and add the remaining 1/2 cup water and the wine. Nest the pan in a bowl of ice or place in the refrigerator until the aspic thickens to the consistency of honey, occasionally stirring gently to prevent air bubbles from developing.

Meanwhile, remove and discard the toothpicks or string from the chicken breasts and place the breasts on a wire rack sitting on a shallow-rimmed tray. Position the decorations--herbs, vegetables, and flowers of choice--on top of the chicken to determine desired pattern, then set the decorations aside. Spoon or brush a thin layer of the thickened wine aspic over the top and sides of the chicken as evenly as possible. When the aspic is slightly tacky, grasp the decorations with tweezers, dip them into the liquid aspic, and place them on the chicken in the selected pattern. Refrigerate, uncovered, until the layer of aspic sets up, about 15 minutes.

Remove the chicken from the refrigerator and cover with a second layer of aspic, coating the decorations as well. It may be necessary to repeat with several layers of aspic, chilling for about 15 minutes between each application, to cover the chicken and decorations completely. The chicken may be served as soon as the final coat of aspic is set or it may be covered with an inverted bowl and refrigerated, for several hours before serving.

To serve, haphazardly chop the 2 reserved hard aspics or cut into tiny cubes with a knife. Arrange the hard aspics on 8 prechilled dinner plates, top with a decorated chicken breast, and serve immediately.

Serves 8 as first course, or 4 to 6 as main course.

INDEX

Recipe Index

ACKNOWLEDGMENTS

To Ed Broussard, Earl Daggett, Ruth Dosher, Gail High, Scottie McKinney, James O. and Lucille McNair, Stephen Marcus, Babs Retzer, Kristi Spence, Margaret Spurlock, and Stephen Suzman for sharing recipes.

To Mary McCoy for cooking nonchicken dinners during my intensive writing period.

To retailers Sue Fisher King in San Francisco and Burt Tessler and Jim Wentworth of Dishes Delmar in San Francisco, and to stylist Maria Winston for the loan of props.

To Gail High for handling the enormous task of keeping the studio kitchen in order when I'm cooking for the camera.

To Patricia Brabant and her assistant Louis Block for superb photography, and for making such hard work fun.

To Cleve Gallat and Chuck Thayer for turning text and photographs into type and pages.

To the entire staff of Chronicle Books for their continued cooperation and good work.

To those special friends who offered encouragement throughout the project, especially John Carr, Louis Hicks, Al Horton, Douglas Jackson, Mark Leno, and Marian May.

To my crew at The Rockpile Press who assist me always in countless ways—Lin Cotton, Addie Prey, Buster Booroo, Joshua J. Chew, and Michael T. Wigglebutt.

Produced by The Rockpile Press, Lake Tahoe and San Francisco

Art direction, book design, and styling by James McNair
Editorial production assistance by Lin Cotton
Photography assistance by Louis Block
Food styling assistance by Gail High
Food styling on pages 92-93 by Scottie McKinney
Background assistance by John Carr, Douglas Jackson, and Mark Leno
Typography and mechanical production by Chuck Thayer and Associates